Frommer's

Boston
day BY day®

4th Edition

by
Leslie Brokaw & Erin Trahan

FrommerMedia LLC

Contents

Published by:

FrommerMedia LLC

Copyright © 2019 FrommerMedia LLC, New York, NY. All rights reserved. No part of this publication may be reproduced, stored in a retrieval system or transmitted in any form or by any means, electronic, mechanical, photocopying, recording, scanning or otherwise, except as permitted under Sections 107 or 108 of the 1976 United States Copyright Act, without the prior written permission of the Publisher. Requests to the Publisher for permission should be addressed to Support@FrommerMedia.com.

Frommer's is a trademark or registered trademark of Arthur Frommer.

ISBN: 978-1-628-87408-2 (paper); 978-1-628-87409-9 (ebk)

Editorial Director: Pauline Frommer
Editor: Lorraine Festa
Production Editor: Heather Wilcox
Photo Editor: Meghan Lamb
Cartographer: Roberta Stockwell
Indexer: Maro Riofrancos

Front cover photos, left to right: Boston skyline over the Boston Commons: © Sean Pavone; ice skating in Frog Pond: © Kwanbenz/Shutterstock.com; Boston Public Garden with its famous duck family statues: © f11photo

Back cover photo: Back Bay Boston skyline: © Galiptynutz

For information on our other products and services, please go to Frommers.com.

Frommer's also publishes its books in a variety of electronic formats. Some content that appears in print may not be available in electronic formats.

5   4   3   2   1

About This Guide

Organizing your time. That's what this guide is all about.

Other guides give you long lists of things to see and do and then expect you to fit the pieces together. The Day by Day guides are different. These guides tell you the best of everything, and then they show you how to see it in the smartest, most time-efficient way. Our authors have designed detailed itineraries organized by time, neighborhood, or special interest. And each tour comes with a bulleted map that takes you from stop to stop.

Hoping to walk in the steps of the Founding Fathers? Or watch a baseball sail over the Green Monster? Or even walk into a bar where everybody knows your name? Whatever your interest or schedule, the Day by Days give you the smartest routes to follow. Not only do we take you to the top attractions, hotels, and restaurants, but we also help you access those special moments that locals get to experience—those "finds" that turn tourists into travelers.

The Day by Days are also your top choice if you're looking for one complete guide for all your travel needs. The best hotels and restaurants for every budget, the greatest shopping values, the wildest nightlife—it's all here.

Why should you trust our judgment? Because our authors personally visit each place they write about. They're an independent lot who say what they think and would never include places they wouldn't recommend to their best friends. They're also open to suggestions from readers. If you'd like to contact them, please send your comments our way at feedback@frommers.com, and we'll pass them on.

Enjoy your Day by Day guide—the most helpful travel companion you can buy. And have the trip of a lifetime.

About the Authors

Leslie Brokaw has worked on over a dozen Frommer's books about Québec and New England. She is an editor for MIT Sloan Management Review and teaches at Emerson College. She and her family live just outside of Boston.

Erin Trahan is a regular contributor to WBUR, Boston's NPR news station, and is a faculty member at Emerson College. She and her family live on Boston's north shore.

An Additional Note

Please be advised that travel information is subject to change at any time—and this is especially true of prices. We therefore suggest that you write or call ahead for confirmation when making your travel plans. The authors, editors, and publisher cannot be held responsible for the experiences of readers while traveling. Your safety is important to us, however, so we encourage you to stay alert and be aware of your surroundings.

Star Ratings, Icons & Abbreviations

Every hotel, restaurant, and attraction listing in this guide has been ranked for quality, value, service, amenities, and special features using a **star-rating system.** Hotels, restaurants, attractions, shopping, and nightlife are rated on a scale of zero stars (recommended) to three stars (exceptional). In addition to the star-rating system, we also use a **kids icon** to point out the best bets for families. Within each tour, we recommend cafes, bars, or restaurants where you can take a break. Each of these stops appears in a shaded box marked with a coffee-cup-shaped bullet ☕.

The following **abbreviations** are used for credit cards:

AE	American Express	MC	MasterCard
DC	Diners Club	V	Visa

Frommers.com

Now that you have this guidebook to help you plan a great trip, visit our website at **www.frommers.com** for additional travel information on more than 3,600 destinations. We update features regularly to give you instant access to the most current trip-planning information available. At Frommers.com, you'll find scoops on the best airfares, lodging rates, and car rental bargains. You can even book your travel online through our reliable travel booking partners. Other popular features include:

- Online updates of our most popular guidebooks

- Vacation sweepstakes and contest giveaways

- Newsletters highlighting the hottest travel trends

- Online travel message boards with featured travel discussions

An Invitation to the Reader

In researching this book, we discovered many wonderful places—hotels, restaurants, shops, and more. We're sure you'll find others. Please tell us about them, so we can share the information with your fellow travelers in upcoming editions. If you were disappointed with a recommendation, we'd love to know that, too. Please write to: Support@FrommerMedia.com.

14 Favorite
Moments

14 Favorite **Moments**

1. Taking in the 360-degree views from the Rose Kennedy Greenway
2. Those first steps into Fenway Park
3. Walking the Freedom Trail
4. Slurping down oysters
5. Slowing down with the Swan Boats in Boston Public Garden
6. Swinging under the stars at the Lawn on D Street
7. Meeting the city's artists and local farmers in SOWA
8. Settling in for a night of theater
9. Strolling under the twinkly white lights of Comm. Ave. in winter
10. Enjoying the Charles River
11. Heading out to the tip of Castle Island to Sullivan's clam shack
12. People watching from a Newbury Street sidewalk café
13. Stepping off the T into Harvard Yard
14. Joining the crowds on Marathon Monday

Previous page: The North End Parks on the Rose Kennedy Greenway.

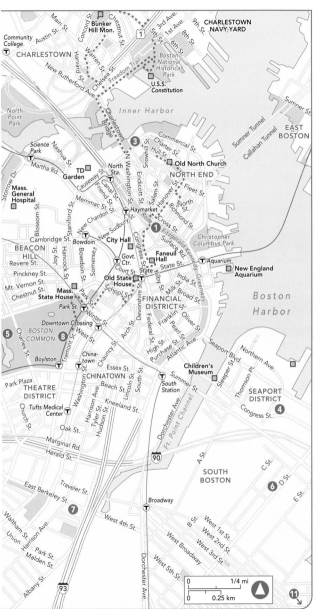

Community College

CHARLESTOWN

Main St.

Austin St.

Harvard St.

Warren St.

Concord St.

Chestnut St.

Bunker Hill Mon.

3rd Ave.
5th St.
1st Ave.
9th St.
8th St.

CHARLESTOWN NAVY YARD

New Rutherford Ave.

Chelsea St.

Freedom Trail

Boston National Historical Park

U.S.S. Constitution

North Point Park

Charlestown Bridge

Inner Harbor

Sumner St.

EAST BOSTON

Sumner Tunnel

Callahan Tunnel

Storrow Dr.

Science Park

Nashua St.

Martha Rd.

Mass. General Hospital

Blossom St.

TD Garden

N. Washington St.

Endicott St.

Commercial St.

Charter St.

Hull St.

N. Margin St.

Salem St.

Snow Hill St.

Old North Church

NORTH END

North Sta.

Causeway St.

Friend St.

Canal St.

Merrimac St.

New Chardon St.

Haymarket

Hanover St.

Fleet St.

North St.

Richmond St.

Cross St.

Fitzgerald Kennedy Surface Rd.

Christopher Columbus Park

Cambridge St.

BEACON HILL

Revere St.

Pinckney St.

Mt. Vernon St.

Chestnut St.

Staniford St.

Bowdoin

Somerset St.

New Sudbury St.

City Hall

Congress St.

Govt. Ctr.

Court St.

State St.

Faneuil Hall

Aquarium

New England Aquarium

India St.

Boston Harbor

Hancock St.

Bowdoin St.

Old State House

Mass. State House

Beacon St.

Park St.

School St.

State St.

Kilby St.

Milk St.

Broad St.

FINANCIAL DISTRICT

Devonshire St.

Franklin St.

Oliver St.

Pearl St.

BOSTON COMMON

Charles St.

Tremont St.

Downtown Crossing

West St.

Winter St.

Chauncy St.

Arch St.

Federal St.

High St.

Purchase St.

Atlantic Ave.

Seaport Blvd.

Northern Ave.

Boylston

Boylston St.

China-town

Essex St.

Beach St.

South St.

Lincoln St.

CHINATOWN

Washington St.

Harrison Ave.

Tyler St.

Hudson St.

Kneeland St.

Summer St.

South Station

Children's Museum

Sleeper St.

Thomson Pl.

SEAPORT DISTRICT

Congress St.

Park Plaza

THEATRE DISTRICT

Church St.

Tufts Medical Center

Oak St.

Marginal Rd.

Herald St.

Dorchester Ave.

Ft. Point Channel

A St.

C St.

D St.

E St.

East Berkeley St.

Traveler St.

Waltham St.

Union Park St.

Harrison Ave.

Malden St.

Albany St.

Broadway

West 4th St.

Dorchester Ave.

West 5th St.

SOUTH BOSTON

B St.

West 1st St.

West 2nd St.

West Broadway

West 3rd St.

0   1/4 mi
0   0.25 km

① ③ ④ ⑤ ⑥ ⑦ ⑧ ⑪

Boston has been a hub of the American experience since its colonial founding in 1630. For centuries it was an engine of U.S. finance and industry. Today it's a fusion of modern life and history. Waves of students pour in each September to attend its colleges and universities, and many stay to work in the region's world-renowned medical and high-tech industries. The result is a cosmopolitan city in a state of continual rejuvenation. Here are 14 favorite moments in this youthful, European-infused city.

Fans take in a Boston Red Sox game at Fenway atop the famed "Green Monster" left field wall.

❶ **Savoring the 360-degree views from the Rose Kennedy Greenway.** Before 2008, an elevated highway dominated the eastern edge of the city. Pedestrians had to pass underneath dark, loud corridors to travel between downtown and the restaurants and hotels along the harbor. When the highway got moved underground, the skies literally opened up. A walkway of connected parks—with food vendors, sculpture, and a carousel—has stitched together this popular part of the city. The change is breathtaking. *See p 29.*

❷ **Taking those first steps into Fenway Park.** Whether it's your first game of the season or the first game of your life at the famed baseball stadium—built in 1912, and the oldest ballpark in major league baseball—emerging from the concrete hallways into the stadium and seeing the expansive sky and emerald green field could make your heart grow two sizes. *See p 18.*

❸ **Walking the Freedom Trail.** A red path—in some stretches brick, in other stretches paint—winds through the streets of old Boston past 16 historic sites of the city's Colonial past. It's a self-guided tour (although tour guides are available) that you can join in at any spot. We provide a map with highlights in this book. *See p 34.*

4 Slurping down oysters. Boston is a seafood town, and good plates of oysters are ubiquitous. Try them at sit-down restaurants like Legal Sea Foods or Row 34 or modest food stalls inside Quincy Market. Wellfleet oysters from Cape Cod deliver a briny taste of the sea. *See p 97.*

5 Slowing down with the Swan Boats in Boston Public Garden. Old-fashioned paddleboats meander the pond (called "the lagoon") in the city's jewel-box garden. Simply watching from the shore can be hypnotic. *See p 90.*

6 Swinging under the stars at the Lawn on D Street. On an urban plot of land between the Seaport District and South Boston, this grassy park has lawn games, food concessions, and occasional live music. Glow-in-the-dark swings the size of truck tires are the big draw at this family-friendly spot. *See p 65.*

7 Meeting the city's artists and local farmers in SoWa. An acronym for "South of Washington" (street), SoWa is a pocket within the South End neighborhood that's rich in art galleries, boutiques, and design showrooms. The seasonal weekend market is a vibrant artistic and local food scene. *See p 80.*

8 Settling in for a night of theater. Exciting contemporary theater is presented at the Huntington Theatre, ArtsEmerson, and the A.R.T. in Cambridge and popular options include Blue Man Group and "Shear Madness." In summer, it's a special treat to pack a blanket and picnic dinner to watch the Commonwealth Shakespeare Company present free Shakespeare on the Boston Common. *See p 121.*

9 Strolling under the twinkling white lights of Comm. Ave. in winter. "Comm. Ave.," the shorthand for Commonwealth Avenue, is the brownstone-lined grand boulevard in the central part of the city. In the cold months, the trees lining a broad pedestrian path in the center of the residential street glitter with thousands of white lights. For a full winter experience, also visit the outdoor ice-skating rink in nearby Boston Common. *See p 17.*

10 Enjoying the Charles River. Boston's major river has paths for

Sailing on the Charles River.

The Boston Marathon, held on Patriots' Day, the third Monday in April, is the world's oldest annual marathon.

walking and biking on both sides and can be viewed from the Red Line subway and from Duck Boat tours. It's especially scenic when sailboats speckle the vista—and when water traffic starts pouring in for the July 4th fireworks celebrations, which take place here. *See p 92.*

⑪ Heading out to the tip of Castle Island to Sullivan's clam shack. To picture this South Boston locale, make your left hand into the "ok" gesture. Your thumbnail is Castle Island, the oldest fortified military site in British North America and now part of the city park system. The space inside your hand is Pleasure Bay, and everything around your hand is ocean. Just adjacent to the park is the famed "Sully's" clam shack. *See p 26.*

⑫ People-watching from a Newbury Street sidewalk cafe. From Arlington Street to Massachusetts Avenue, the European-feeling Newbury Street, with beautifully maintained brownstones and bustling sidewalks, is a central destination for sophisticated shopping, strolling, and noshing. *See p 18.*

⑬ Stepping off the T into Harvard Yard. The city of Cambridge is just across the Charles River from Boston, and Harvard University, in Cambridge, is an easy subway ride from Boston's downtown. The school's bucolic central quad is known as Harvard Yard, and open to all visitors. *See p 70.*

⑭ Joining the crowds on Marathon Monday. The Boston Marathon takes place in April on an obscure Boston public holiday called Patriots' Day. It's a terrifically festive day. True locals start the morning with a "coffee regulah" (meaning with cream and sugar) at "Dunkies," slang for locally based Dunkin' Donuts. *See p 158.* ●

1 The Best Full-Day Tours

The Best in One Day

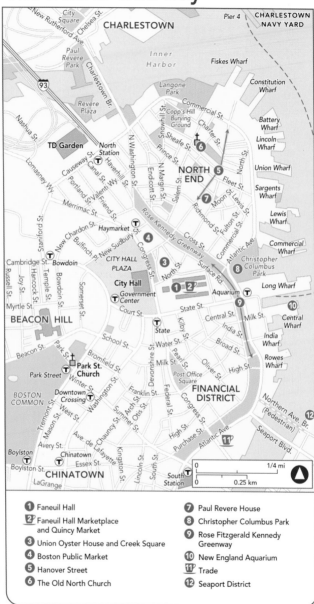

1 Faneuil Hall
2 Faneuil Hall Marketplace and Quincy Market
3 Union Oyster House and Creek Square
4 Boston Public Market
5 Hanover Street
6 The Old North Church

7 Paul Revere House
8 Christopher Columbus Park
9 Rose Fitzgerald Kennedy Greenway
10 New England Aquarium
11 Trade
12 Seaport District

Previous page: Boston's famed Faneuil Hall.

Center your first day in Boston around the contours of the harbor and waterfront, where old meets new. You'll start at Faneuil Hall, a marketplace and a meeting hall for over 275 years, and you'll follow part of the Freedom Trail, exploring some of the city's rich political history. This tour winds through Boston's Italian North End neighborhood, home to the Paul Revere House and the Old North Church, and south to the newly thriving Seaport District. START: **T to Government Center, then walk down the wide staircase to Faneuil Hall Marketplace.**

❶ ★ **kids** **Faneuil Hall.** Many of the great orators of America's colonial past inspired audiences to rebellion here, earning the building the nickname "the cradle of liberty." One of the best-known speakers was the revolutionary firebrand Samuel Adams, whose statue stands at the entrance on the Congress Street side of the building. Originally erected in 1742, Faneuil Hall was a gift from prominent merchant Peter Faneuil (whose trade included enslaved people from Africa in addition to sugar, molasses, and timber). A $3.8 million renovation project in early 2018 provided needed upgrades to the building's heating and accessibility. National Park Service rangers staff the first-floor visitor center and give brief talks in the second-floor Great Hall auditorium. ⏱ *10 min.; 30 min. for tour. Dock Square at Congress St.* ☎ *617/242-5601. www.nps.gov/ bost. Free admission. Daily 9am–5pm (visitor center until 6pm). T: Government Center or Haymarket.*

❷ With shops, restaurants (such as Durgin-Park, p 104), food stalls, jugglers, and musicians, the 5-building **Faneuil Hall Marketplace and Quincy Market** complex is a good place to gravitate to for a meal or people-watching. The Quincy Market building holds a huge food court with vendors such as Boston Chowda Co., Steve's

Greek Cuisine, and North End Bakery (with savory arancini [stuff rice balls] in addition to sweet treats). Public restrooms are on the lower level. ⏱ *30 min. Bordered by State, Congress & North sts. & Atlantic Ave.* ☎ *617/523-1300. www.faneuil hallmarketplace.com. Daily 10am– 9pm; restaurants may open earlier & close later.*

❸ ★ **Union Oyster House and Creek Square.** One block north of Faneuil Hall are some of the oldest and most atmospheric lanes in Boston. As you face the Samuel Adams statue in front of Fanueil Hall, turn left to begin walking up Union Street. This street is part of the Freedom Trail, a sidewalk path marked by red bricks or red paint, which passes historic sites throughout the city. (A walking tour of the full Freedom Trail is presented on p 34.) The glass sculptures on your left are the **New England Holocaust Memorial** (p 38). On your right, at #41, is the oldest restaurant in Boston and "the oldest restaurant in continuous service in the U.S.": **Union Oyster House** (p 109). It opened in 1826 and has a small gift shop. Take a peek down the adjacent Marshall Street for a look back in time: The narrow lane and brick facades are reminiscent of 19th-century England and lead to the teeny Creek Square intersection a block down. ⏱ *5 min. 41 Union St. & the adjacent Marshall St.*

Take a break at a North End cafe to enjoy some cannoli and a cappuccino.

☎ 617/227-2750. www.unionoyster house.com. $$. T: Haymarket.

④ ★★ Boston Public Market. New in 2015, this indoor market has given local farmers a permanent downtown home and consumers a year-round market. Vendors include **Union Square Donuts** (its maple bacon donut is a standout); **Taza Chocolate** (with both iced and hot chocolate drinks), **Boston Smoked Fish Company** (whose haddock is smoked at the Boston Fish Pier); and **Red Apple Farm** (featuring cider from Massachusetts apples). You can get food to eat here or to take out. ⏱ 20 min. 100 Hanover St. ☎ 617/973-4909. www.bostonpublic market.org. Mon–Sat 8am–8pm, Sun 10am–8pm. T: Haymarket.

⑤ ★★ kids Hanover Street. This lively street is at the heart of the North End, Boston's most prominent Italian-American neighborhood. Most afternoons and evenings it overflows with locals and out-of-towners enjoying its restaurants and cafes. Increasingly sophisticated retail options include quirky boutiques both here and on the parallel **Salem Street,** as well as

some of the side streets that connect them. Explore a bit and consider settling down with a cappuccino and cannoli. Popular destinations are **Caffè Vittoria** at 290–296 Hanover St. (☎ 617/227-7606; www.caffevittoria.com; $) and **Mike's Pastry,** 300 Hanover St. (☎ 617/742-3050; www.mikes pastry.com; $). ⏱ 15 min. T: Haymarket.

⑥ ★★★ kids The Old North Church. A National Historic Landmark, founded in 1722, this church—whose formal name is Christ Church—has an interior of boxy pews with high seats, better to capture the heat from the bricks that early congregants would carry in with them. In 1775, it was here that sexton Robert Newman hung two signal lanterns to alert Paul Revere and Williams Dawes that "the British are coming." The complex today has small gardens and a gift shop. ⏱ 40 min. 193 Salem St. ☎ 617/858-8231. www.oldnorth. com. $8 adults, $6 seniors & students, $4 kids. Talks (5–7 min.) are available by educators & there are online supplements & games for self-guided tours. 30-min. Behind the Scenes tour & 40-min. Bones & Burials tour daily Mar–Dec; check website for times. Both tours $6 adults, $5 students/seniors/military, $4 children (Bones tour not suitable for children under 13). T: Haymarket.

⑦ ★★★ kids Paul Revere House. A visit to the home of "midnight rider" Paul Revere provides a rich sense of what daily life was like for a successful colonial craftsman. Outfitted with 17th- and 18th-century furniture and artifacts, including silver pieces created by Revere himself, this small wood structure is open for self-guided tours. See p 38 for additional details. ⏱ 30 min. 19 North Sq.

This home, built in 1680, was owned by Paul Revere from 1770 to 1800 and opened as a museum in 1908.

☎ 617/523-2338. www.paulrevere house.org. $5 adults, $4.50 seniors & students, $1 kids 5–17, free for kids 4 & under. Apr 15–Oct 31 daily 9:30am–5:15pm; Nov 1–Apr 14 daily 9:30am–4:15pm. Closed Mon Jan–Mar. T: Haymarket.

❽ ★ kids Christopher Columbus Park. This small harborside park is a welcome green spot. It includes a tot lot / jungle gym for smaller children, a fountain spray park, benches and lawn for lounging, a circular performance area that occasionally has musicians, and a dramatic central trellis draped with wisteria vines in warm weather and blue lights in winter. ⏱ 10 min. 110 Atlantic Ave., adjacent to Long Wharf. www.cityofboston.gov/parks. Free. Open 24 hr. T: Aquarium.

❾ ★★★ kids Rose Fitzgerald Kennedy Greenway. A raised highway dominated this part of the city until 2008. Pedestrians would pass beneath its rumbling dark arches to get from downtown to the harbor area. But the "Big Dig" public works project moved I-93 underground, and a much-welcome walkway of connected parks filled in the scar where the highway once stood. The park is 1½ miles long and includes, at its the northern end, a lovely Carousel (open year-round, subject to weather), fountains (including the family-friendly Rings Fountain with jet sprays to play in), the Trillian Garden beer-garden (corner of High Street & Atlantic Avenue; closed in winter), and sculptures, murals, and other engaging public artwork. Food

Boston's Freedom Trail

Only a handful of U.S. cities have histories as rich and varied as Boston's. A walk along the Freedom Trail, a 2½-mile path through downtown, covers many of the highlights and allows visitors to tread in the footsteps of the country's Founding Fathers. See p 34 for the tour "Freedom Trail."

trucks dot the cross streets. The Greenway concludes near the central transport terminal South Station, at the city's financial district. Directly across the harbor from this end of the Greenway is the Seaport District, accessible by foot on Seaport Boulevard, Congress Street, or Summer Street. The Greenway's namesake, Rose Kennedy, was the mother of U.S. President John F. Kennedy. ① *30 min. Alongside Atlantic Ave. & Cross St. www.rose kennedygreenway.org. Free. Open 24 hr. T: Aquarium.*

⓾ ★★★ kids **New England Aquarium.** The centerpiece of this well-appointed and popular aquarium is the 4-story **Giant Ocean Tank,** which contains sea turtles, sharks, hundreds of colorful reef fishes, and 200,000 gallons of water—check out the live webcam at www.neaq.org/giant-ocean-tank-web-cam. The surrounding displays and hands-on exhibits are home to other sea creatures, including seahorses the size of grapes. Seals and sea lions frolic in the open-air marine mammal center, and there's a ray touch tank, where visitors can pet the exhibit's leathery-skinned inhabitants. More than 80 penguins greet visitors just inside the front entrance. Even in you don't go in, you can still visit the Atlantic harbor seals, whose tank is outside next to the front doors. ① *2 hr. 1 Central Wharf, ½ block from State St. & Atlantic Ave. ☎ 617/973-5200. www.neaq.org. Admission $28 adults, $26 seniors, $19 kids 3–11, free for kids under 3. IMAX theater tickets $10 adults, $8 seniors & kids. Tickets are available online in advance. Open July–Aug Sun–Thurs 9am–6pm, Fri–Sat 9am–7pm; Sept–June Mon–Fri 9am–5pm, Sat–Sun 9am–6pm. T: Aquarium.*

Dewey Square Park in Rose Fitzgerald Kennedy Greenway.

Penguin exhibit at the New England Aquarium.

11 Chef Jody Adams presents Mediterranean food and cocktails in the upscale, elegant **Trade,** which anchors this busy corner near the financial district. Select a spread of small plates to share tapas-style, such as Aleppo grilled shrimp, lamb sausage flatbread, and anything with muhammara, a tasty spread made from red pepper, pomegranate molasses, and walnuts. Adams' Baked Alaska, featuring mango sorbet, is worth the trip alone. *540 Atlantic Ave. See p 117.*

12 ★ kids **Seaport District.** Boston's newly hot neighborhood has been the long-time home of the **Boston World Trade Center** and the **Boston Convention and Exhibition Center.** If you are traveling with children, head to the stellar **Boston Children's Museum,** a three-story playground of activities geared to kids up to age 10 (p 29). Otherwise, consider a trip to the **Institute of Contemporary Art** (p 64) or any of the excellent restaurants that have sprung up in the neighborhood in the last few years, including **Row 34** (p 108). A tour of this neighborhood on p 62 picks up where this tour ends. *T: Courthouse.*

The Best in Two Days

1. MIT and Kendall Square
2. Charles Street
3. Louisberg Square
4. Tatte Bakery & Café
5. Boston Public Garden
6. George Washington Statue
7. Commonwealth Avenue Mall
8. Newbury Street
9. Piattini Wine Cafe
10. Trident Booksellers and Café
11. Copley Square
12. Fenway Park

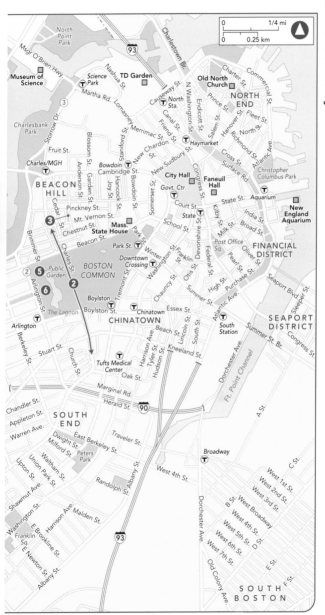

After getting a taste of the way Boston blends the old with the new, settle in for a look at classic Boston and its colonial legacy. In the 19th century, the city grew westward, building up the neighborhoods called Beacon Hill and Back Bay. This tour focuses less on specific sites and more on the evocative, thriving neighborhoods of the city, where you can take in the full pulse of Boston life. START: **T to Kendall.**

The "Salt and Pepper Bridge" (real name: Longfellow Bridge), with its namesake towers.

1 ★ MIT and Kendall Square. The Massachusetts Institute of Technology, one of the most prestigious institutes of higher education in the world, is based in Cambridge just across the Charles River from Boston. Its campus runs along the river between the Longfellow Bridge and Massachusetts Avenue Bridge. If you start a tour of the city on the Cambridge side of the river and walk across the Longfellow back into Boston, you get an expansive, glorious view of the city skyline. This bridge is nicknamed the Salt and Pepper Bridge because of the towers, which look like spice shakers. It has been under renovation since 2015 and is slated for completion late 2018. If the weather is poor, start the tour at **2** Charles Street. ○ *20 min. T: Kendall.*

2 ★★ Charles Street. Charles Street between the Longfellow Bridge and the Boston Common isn't very long—little more than ⅓ of a mile—but it's one of the prettiest streets in the city. It's lined with 3- and 4-story brick buildings and chock-a-block with boutiques and gift shops. Stroll slowly and look around to take in the heart of the Beacon Hill residential neighborhood. We offer a detailed tour of Beacon Hill and Back Bay on p 56. ○ *20 min. T: Charles/MGH.*

3 ★ Louisberg Square. East of Charles Street, up 2 short blocks on either of the side streets Pinckney or Mt. Vernon, is Louisberg Square, a leafy oasis and one of Boston's most prestigious residential pockets. An Italian marble likeness of Athenian statesman Aristides anchors one end of the private park at the square's center, the common property of the Louisburg Square Proprietors, believed to be the oldest homeowners' association in the country. The 22 houses that rim the elegant square were built between 1834 and 1848. ⏱ *15 min. T: Charles/MGH.*

4 Cozy and bright **Tatte Bakery & Café** is a perfect place to relax with a pistachio croissant, avocado tartine with peppery arugula, or perhaps a sweet potato tarte Tatin. Breakfast, lunch, and dinner are served weekdays and brunch is offered all day Friday through Sunday at this outpost of the small regional chain, which has eight locations around Greater Boston. In nice weather, try to snag an outdoor table. *70 Charles St.* ☎ *617/723-5555. www.tattebakery. com. $.*

5 ★★★ **kids** **Boston Public Garden.** Boston's most beloved park is a perfect place to unwind. The Public Garden overflows with seasonal blooms and permanent plantings (the roses, which peak in June, are particularly lovely). No matter how crowded it gets, it feels serene. A small lagoon in the center, surrounded by weeping willows, is home to ducks and swans in warm weather and the slow-moving, iconic Swan Boats. For more details about this gem of a park, see p 53. ⏱ *15 min. Bordered by Arlington, Boylston, Charles & Beacon sts. www.friendsofthepublic garden.org. Free admission. Daily dawn–dusk. T: Arlington.*

6 ★★ **George Washington Statue.** Boston's first equestrian statue guards the most dramatic entrance to the city's loveliest park. The 38-foot-tall statue is considered an excellent likeness of the first president, who was an outstanding horseman. The artist, Thomas Ball, was a Charlestown native who worked in Italy. Among his students was noted sculptor Daniel Chester French, who created the Lincoln Memorial in Washington, D.C. *Inside the Boston Public Garden, at the corner of Arlington St. & Commonwealth Ave. T: Arlington.*

7 ★ **kids** **Commonwealth Avenue Mall.** The centerpiece of architect Arthur Gilman's

The 38-foot-tall statue of George Washington overlooks the most dramatic entrance to the Boston Public Garden.

French-inspired design of the Back Bay is this dramatic boulevard, 240 feet wide with a 100-foot-wide tree-lined path down the center. Construction began in 1858, and by the late 1870s, it was important enough for landscape architect Frederick Law Olmsted to include it in his system of Boston parks known as the Emerald Necklace. Beautiful buildings line both sides of the street: As the landfill that created the neighborhood marched west, architectural styles grew wilder, leaving behind a few stretches where it hardly seems possible that the building facades could hold more ornamentation—gables, archways, medallions, fanciful wrought iron, and ornamental brickwork. A curious collection of statues flanks the mall, beginning with Alexander Hamilton across Arlington Street from George Washington. In winter, its trees are decorated with small white lights, making this one of the most beautifully atmospheric passages of the city. ○ 15 min. Commonwealth Ave., starting at Arlington St. & extending west. T: Arlington.

⑧ ★★★ kids **Newbury Street.** Parallel to "Comm. Ave." and one block south, Newbury Street is the best-known retail destination in New England and has something for everyone. It's famous for art galleries, designer boutiques, and sidewalk cafes, although its unique personality has admittedly been watered down by the influx of generic national chains. Like Commonwealth Avenue, Newbury starts at the Public Garden and extends west. The stores and restaurants nearest to the Garden have higher price tags, and venues become moderately less expensive and quirkier block to block. There are three T stops within a block of Newbury, including Copley Square near the middle. See p 82 for

shopping highlights. ○ 45 min. Newbury St. from Arlington St. to Massachusetts Ave. www.newbury streetleague.org. T: Arlington, Copley, or Hynes Convention Center.

Most of the pasta, panini, and pizzas dishes at ⑨ **Piattini Wine Cafe** are $10 at lunch, and there are appealing outdoor cafe tables along the street. Three blocks further on Newbury, ⑩ **Trident Booksellers and Café** is a great option for vegetarian food or all-day breakfast. It offers a huge selection of omelets, breakfast burritos, challah French toast, and grain bowls—plus tea, coffee, beer, and wine. It's a perfect place to linger. Piattini: 226 Newbury St. See p 108. Trident: 338 Newbury St. ☎ 617/267-8688. www.tridentbooks cafe.com. See p. 80. $.

⑪ ★★ **Copley Square.** One block south of Newbury Street is the parallel Boylston Street, and the heart of the city is here, between Clarendon and Dartmouth streets. Copley Square is an open plaza bookended by the granite **Trinity Church** and all-glass **John Hancock Tower** on the east and the **Boston Public Library** on the west. The **BosTix Booth** for discount theater tickets is here on the west side (p 131). An architectural tour of the buildings of the square and important nearby churches is on p 40. ○ 30 min. T: Copley.

⑫ ★★★ kids **Fenway Park.** If you're only in Boston for one day, and if the Red Sox are playing in town, by all means try to get tickets. Boston lives and breathes sports, especially baseball, and is fiercely proud of its stadium. Fenway is as wonderfully old-timey as you're going to get in pro sports today, with a facility that has

The Commonwealth Avenue Mall.

received only modest renovations since its construction in 1912. It has live organ accompaniment and an enthusiastic hometown crowd. True, tickets are among the most expensive in all of major league baseball. Still, settling in for a game with a couple of Fenway Franks and cold brews is one of the ultimate Boston experiences. The 37,731-seat capacity stadium is right in the city and walking distance from Copley Square—a little over a mile to the west, through safe and busy areas. Tours of the stadium are available daily year-round if it's not possible to see to a game—see p 32.
🕐 *Hours & hours. 4 Jersey St. (formerly Yawkey Way). www.mlb.com/redsox/ballpark. Game tickets $10–$650. Fenway Park tour $14–$50. T: Kenmore.*

The Best **in Three Days**

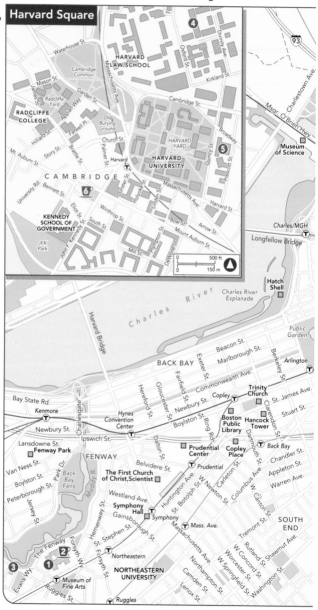

Harvard Square

Waterhouse St.

HARVARD
LAW SCHOOL

Oxford St.

Divinity Ave.

93

Mason St.

Cambridge
Common

Garden St.

Kirkland St.

James St.

Radcliffe
Yard

RADCLIFFE
COLLEGE

Appian Way

Farwell Pl.

Old
Burying
Ground

Cambridge St.

Msgr. O'Brien Hwy.

Charlestown Ave.

Museum
of Science

Hilliard St.

Story St.

Brattle St.

Church St.

Palmer St.

HARVARD
YARD

HARVARD
UNIVERSITY

Broadway

Mt. Auburn St.

Harvard

CAMBRIDGE

Dunster St.

Holyoke St.

Linden St.

Massachusetts Ave.

Prescott St.

Harvard St.

Charles/MGH

University Rd.

Bennett St.

Eliot St.

Winthrop St.

Bow St.

Arrow St.

Longfellow Bridge

KENNEDY
SCHOOL OF
GOVERNMENT

South St.

Plympton St.

Mount Auburn St.

JFK
Park

John F. Kennedy St.

Mill St.

DeWolfe St.

0   500 ft
0   150 m

Charles River

Charles River
Esplanade

Hatch
Shell

Harvard Bridge

Charles River

Public
Garden

Beacon St.

BACK BAY

Marlborough St.

Berkeley St.

Arlington

Bay State Rd.

Kenmore

Charlesgate

Exeter St.

Fairfield St.

Gloucester St.

Hereford St.

Commonwealth Ave.

Copley

Trinity
Church

St. James Ave.

Clarendon St.

Stuart St.

Newbury St.

Boston
Public
Library

Hancock
Tower

Hynes
Convention
Center

Ring Rd.

Dartmouth St.

Boylston St.

Newbury St.

Ipswich St.

Dalton St.

Lansdowne St.

Fenway Park

FENWAY

Back
Bay
Fens

Muddy R.

Belvidere St.

The First Church
of Christ, Scientist

Prudential
Center

Prudential

Copley
Place

Back Bay

Chandler St.

Appleton St.

Warren Ave.

Van Ness St.

Park Dr.

Boylston St.

Peterborough St.

Jersey St.

Westland Ave.

Symphony
Hall

Gainsborough St.

Symphony

Huntington Ave.

St. Botolph St.

W. Newton St.

Carleton St.

Columbus Ave.

Canton St.

SOUTH
END

Tremont St.

W. Concord St.

Rutland St.

W. Springfield St.

Hemenway St.

St. Stephen St.

Mass. Ave.

Massachusetts Ave.

W. Worcester St.

Shawmut Ave.

Washington St.

The Fenway

Forsyth Wy.

Northeastern

Forsyth St.

Evans Wy.

Museum
of Fine Arts

Ruggles St.

NORTHEASTERN
UNIVERSITY

Northampton St.

Camden St.

Lenox St.

Ruggles

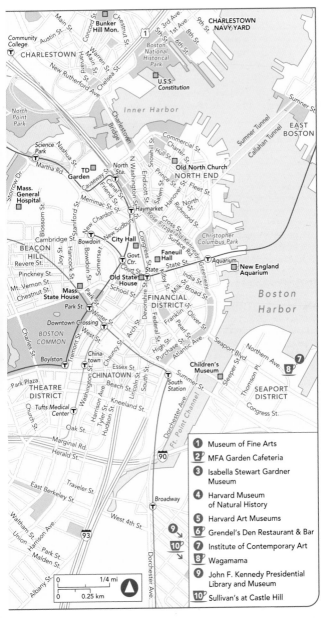

1 Museum of Fine Arts
2 MFA Garden Cafeteria
3 Isabella Stewart Gardner Museum
4 Harvard Museum of Natural History
5 Harvard Art Museums
6 Grendel's Den Restaurant & Bar
7 Institute of Contemporary Art
8 Wagamama
9 John F. Kennedy Presidential Library and Museum
10 Sullivan's at Castle Hill

After two days of walking, take some time to visit the city's rich cultural and artistic highlights. The listings below are the city's most prominent options. Boston's major institution is its Museum of Fine Arts, and a block away is a spectacular gem, the Isabella Stewart Gardner Museum, housed in Mrs. Gardner's Venetian-styled palazzo. Harvard University's museums are a subway ride away in the heart of Cambridge, the stimulating Institute of Contemporary Art is next to the harbor in the Seaport District, and the official presidential library of John F. Kennedy is on the southern end of the city in Dorchester. START: **T to Museum of Fine Arts.**

❶ ★★★ kids **Museum of Fine Arts.** The familiar and the undiscovered meet here creating an irresistible atmosphere that makes the MFA one of the best art museums in the world. You can take a mobile guide, concentrate on a particular period, or head straight to one specific piece. The vast permanent collection soars from classical to contemporary, prints to photography, musical instruments to textiles. The Impressionism gallery includes Gauguin's masterpiece *Where Do We Come From? What Are We? Where Are We Going?*, the Degas sculpture *Little Fourteen-Year-Old Dancer*, Van Gogh's *Houses at Auvers*, plus works by Cézanne, Pissarro, Signac, and Sisley, and an entire gallery devoted to Monet.

The MFA itself is an architectural landmark; the heart of the original building (1909) is the rotunda, accessed from a sweeping staircase. It holds one of the museum's signature elements, John Singer Sargent's Rotunda Murals, which depict mythological figures such as Apollo, Athena, the Muses, and Prometheus. Later additions to the facility were also completed with a splash: The Linde Family Wing for Contemporary Art was designed by I. M. Pei (1981), and the Art of the Americas wing (2010) is the work of Sir Norman Foster and his firm, Foster + Partners.

Mary Cassatt's In the Loge, *at the Museum of Fine Arts.*

The 2010 renovation gave the museum a central, glass-enclosed 63-foot tall atrium, complete with a cafe (one of five of dining options) and a 42½-foot-high lime green glass tower by Dale Chihuly. In addition to being a central gathering space, the courtyard connects the new wing to the historic building.

Three don't-miss paintings, which are deeply Boston in subject matter and much beloved: John Singleton Copley's iconic portrait of

Paul Revere (1768) John Singer Sargent's *Daughters of Edward Darley Boit* (1882); and Childe Hassam's *At Dusk (Boston Common at Twilight)* (1885-86).

🕐 At least 2 hr. 465 Huntington Ave. ☎ 617/267-9300. www.mfa.org. Admission (good for 2 visits within 10 days) $25 adults, $23 seniors & students, $10 kids 7–17 on school days before 3pm, otherwise free. Free for kids 6 & under. Voluntary contribution Wed 4–9:45pm. Mobile guides, featuring audio, video & images, can be rented for $6 adults, $4 kids 17 & under. Check the website for hotels that offer package deals that include museum admission. Sat–Tues 10am–5pm, Wed–Fri 10am–10pm. Closed on major holidays (check website). T: Museum of Fine Arts.

The MFA has some fancy dining options, including the **New American Café** in the central atrium and the cafe and wine bar **Taste** near the Remis Auditorium. But the 2️⃣ **MFA Garden Cafeteria** is a good option for a more modest, healthy, and fast meal, and has lots of tables for families and groups. It has a decent salad bar along with the expected sandwiches, burgers, pizza, and soup. *Located in the MFA's Linde Family Wing for Contemporary Art on the ground floor. $.*

3️⃣ ★★★ kids **Isabella Stewart Gardner Museum.** An heiress and socialite, Gardner (1840–1924) was also an avid traveler and patron of the arts. The core of the museum is her private collection of paintings, sculpture, furniture, tapestries, and decorative objects. The largest work of art, though, is the building itself, completed in 1901 and designed to resemble a 15th-century Venetian palace. Three floors of galleries surround the plant- and flower-filled courtyard, making the space one of the most unlikely and gorgeous in the city. Galleries feature works by Titian, Botticelli, Raphael, Rembrandt, Matisse, and

The Isabella Stewart Gardner Museum courtyard is the centerpiece of the museum, designed to resemble a 15th-century Venetian palace.

John Singer Sargent's 1888 portrait of Isabella Stewart Gardner.

Sargent—whose monumental *El Jaleo*, a painting of a Gypsy dancer and her musicians, takes up an entire wall in the museum's Spanish Cloister. A glass-enclosed wing, designed by Renzo Piano, debuted in 2012 and is a treasure in its own right. (Piano termed it the "respectful nephew to the great aunt.") It includes the lovely Café G (open Wed–Mon; museum tickets not required) and a concert space, Calderwood Hall. The museum has an unfortunate claim to fame: An art heist in 1990 of important works by Rembrandt, Vermeer, and Degas was estimated to be worth more than $500 million, making it the single largest property theft in the world. As of 2018, the case remains unsolved, and the museum has empty frames in the locations where the art once was displayed, "as a placeholder for the missing works and as symbols of hope awaiting their return," it says. One last fact: Gardner was a big Red Sox fan, and in honor of that passion the museum offers $2 off adult and senior admission to visitors wearing Red Sox paraphernalia. ⏱ *2 hr. 25 Evans Way.* ☎ *617/566-1401.*

www.gardnermuseum.org. Admission $15 adults, $12 seniors, $5 students, free for kids 17 & under, military & families & adults named Isabella with ID. Wed–Mon 11am–5pm (until 9pm Thurs). T: Museum of Fine Arts.

④ ★★ kids **Harvard Museum of Natural History.** The most-visited of Harvard's attractions, the museum has dinosaurs—including a Triceratops skull the size of a toddler and a 42-foot-long prehistoric marine reptile—plus a spectacular Great Mammal Hall with land creatures behind glass at floor level and giant whale skeletons overhead, and a room of incredible sparkling gemstones including a 1,600-pound amethyst geode from Brazil. Also here are the world-famous Blaschka Glass Flowers, 4,300 vividly realistic models of flowers, leaves, and other plants created by the father and son team Leopold and Rudolf Blaschka, from Dresden, Germany. The gallery that houses many of the glass models was given an extensive renovation in 2016 including repair and cleaning of the items, and many nearly glow now. The museum is just the right size for families with curious children, and a small gift shop has a smart collection of fun and educational items. Note that the galleries are on the building's third floor (up 51 steps) and that the main entrance is not wheelchair-accessible. The North Entrance, on the left side of the building, is fully accessible and has an elevator. ⏱ *2 hr. 26 Oxford St.* ☎ *617/495-3045. www.hmnh. harvard.edu. Admission $12 adults, $10 seniors & students, $8 kids 3–18, free for kids 2 & under; free for Massachusetts residents year-round Sun 9am–noon & Sept–May Wed 3–5pm. Daily 9am–5pm. T: Harvard.*

⑤ ★★ kids **Harvard Art Museums.** Three institutions make up the Harvard Art Museums—the Fogg Museum, focused on Western arts; the Busch-Reisinger Museum, with art from central and northern Europe, especially Germany; and the Arthur M. Sackler Museum, dedicated to art from Asia, the Middle East, and the Mediterranean. A 6-year, $350 million renovation and expansion, completed in 2014, united the three museums under one roof and added a shop and a cafe (both open to the public without museum admission) as well as a 300-seat lecture hall. The facility is just outside the walls of Harvard Yard on its east side. ⏱ *2 hr. 32 Quincy St.* ☎ *617/495-9400. www.harvardartmuseums.org. Admission $15 adults, $13 seniors, $10 students, free for kids 17 & under. Daily 10am–5pm. T: Harvard.*

In the heart of Harvard Square at the corner of the small Winthrop Square park, 🖟 **Grendel's Den Restaurant & Bar** has been around since 1971 and serves up tasty, affordable pub grub. Cozy and comfortable, it's a Harvard Square classic. There's always a daily lunch special for $6. *89 Winthrop St. See p 105.*

🕖 ★★ kids **Institute of Contemporary Art.** Boston's first new art museum in almost a century opened in 2006 (the institution dates to 1936). Its horizon-broadening definition of art encompasses everything from painting and sculpture to film. The collection includes 68 major works of 20th- and 21st-century art by women, including Kara Walker, Cindy Sherman, Cornelia Parker, Tara Donovan, and Louise Bourgeois. The performance theater hosts an eclectic array of programs, from jazz piano and spoken prose to dance and world music concerts. The upper levels of the building jut out toward the harbor, providing breathtaking views. There's an excellent gift shop. ⏱ *2 hr. 100 Northern Ave.* ☎ *617/478-3100. www.icaboston.org. Admission $15 adults, $13 seniors, $10 students, free for kids 17 & under; free to all Thurs after 5pm. Tues–Sun & some Mon holidays 10am–5pm (until 9pm Thurs–Fri; until 5pm first Fri of the month). T: Courthouse.*

The Seaport locale of the London-based, pan-Asian 🕗 **Wagamama** opened in 2017 and is a welcome expansion. Most seating is at long communal tables. Prices are a bit steep—$17 for ramen—but portions tend to be large, and the bowls are packed with fresh veggies and your choice of protein. If you're stumped by the menu, a good go-to is the ginger chicken udon, which has chicken, snow peas, egg, chilies, bean sprouts, pickled ginger, and cilantro atop chewy udon noodles. Lunch and dinner daily. *100 Northern Ave., behind the ICA.* ☎ *617/933-9304. www.wagamama.us. $$. T: Courthouse.*

🕘 ★★ kids **John F. Kennedy Presidential Library and Museum.** Copious collections of memorabilia, photos, and audio and video recordings illustrate the exhibits here, which capture the 35th president in vibrant style. Visits start with a 17-minute film about his early life narrated by Kennedy himself, using cleverly edited audio clips. Displays start with the 1960 presidential campaign and proceed chronologically, ending in a dim room where news reports of his assassination play. ⏱ *2 hr. Columbia Point, near UMass Boston.* ☎ *866/JFK-1960 or* ☎ *617/514-1600. www.jfklibrary.org. Admission*

I. M. Pei designed the Kennedy library to suit its location on Dorchester Bay.

$14 adults; $12 seniors & college students with ID; $10 youth 13–17; free for kids 12 & under. Daily 9am–5pm (start time for last introductory film of the day is at 3:55pm). T: JFK/ UMass, then free shuttle bus.

Finish out your three days in Boston in one last neighborhood and one final culinary station. Castle Island in South Boston is the oldest fortified military site in British North America, with the first fort built here in 1643. It's now part of Boston park system. It's also no longer an island, thanks to the development of causeways and roadways on top of them, although it's still mostly surrounded by water. Next to the park is 🔟 **Sullivan's at Castle Hill,** better known as "Sully's." It's a 1951 clam shack where fried clams and hot dogs are a harbinger of summer. Lobster rolls here, which locals travel for, are $15. Open daily late February to late November, but call to confirm hours when the weather is iffy and in spring and fall. Stroll with your food to aptly named Pleasure Bay to take in some ocean air in the final hours of your Boston visit. *2080 Day Boulevard, South Boston.* ☎ *617/268-5685. www. sullivanscastleisland.com. $.* ●

The Best Special-Interest Tours

Boston with Kids

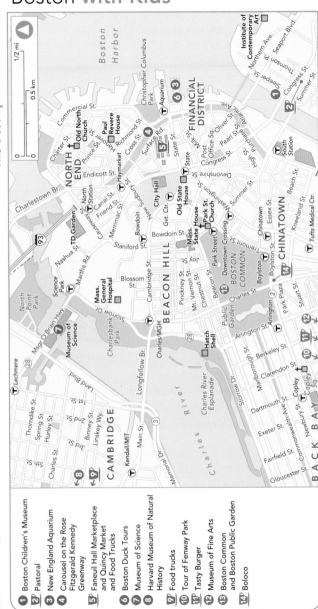

1 Boston Children's Museum
2 Pastoral
3 New England Aquarium
4 Carousel on the Rose Fitzgerald Kennedy Greenway
5 Faneuil Hall Marketplace and Quincy Market
6 Boston Duck Tours
7 Museum of Science
8 Harvard Museum of Natural History
9 Food trucks
10 Tour of Fenway Park
11 Tasty Burger
12 Museum of Fine Arts
13 Boston Common and Boston Public Garden
14 Boloco

Previous page: Boston Duck Tours cruise the Charles River.

Not only is Boston a great "college town," given the 150,000 or so students who attend its 50-plus colleges and universities each year, but it's also a great city for children. World-class kid-centric museums cater to a range of interests, and there are engaging outdoor options both by land and by sea—literally. You know your kids, you know their interests. So rather than provide a prescriptive list of places to visit in order, consider this "tour" a "best of" collection of options.

1 ★★★ kids **Boston Children's Museum.** For kids under 11 or so—though the sweet spot is ages 1 to 7—this is one of the best play spaces in the city. Kids shake it on an illuminated dance floor, work in a "construction" area, play grocery store in a bodega in the "Boston Black" wing, create giant soap bubbles, explore the laws of motion by making golf balls do loop de loops along ramps, visit a Japanese house, and scramble along a three-story maze. And that's only a tenth of the options. **The Boston Tea Party Museum** (p 63), housed in part on a restored 18th-century ship, is across the Fort Point Channel from the Children's Museum entrance and an option for older children. ① *3–5 hr. 308 Congress St., overlooking Fort Point Channel.* ☎ *617/426-6500. www.bostonchildrensmuseum.org. Admission $17 (adults & children), free for kids under age 1; $1 Fri 5–9pm. Sat–Thurs 10am–5pm, Fri 10am–9pm. T: South Station & 10-min. walk, or Courthouse.*

The Boston Children's Museum offers interactive play on three floors.

2 A block from the Children's Museum, **Pastoral** is fancy enough to feel special and accommodating enough that you can show up with kids. There are over a dozen artisan pizza options and gluten-free pasta, too. A long beer and wine list tilts Italian. *345 Congress St. See p 108.*

3 ★★★ kids **New England Aquarium.** Big enough to

comfortably accommodate the masses of school groups that descend upon this popular attraction, the aquarium is a delight to small children, grandparents, and everyone in between. A wide ramp travels up and around a massive central tank with sea turtles, sharks, eels, and reef fishes, with exhibits tucked off in every direction. Tickets can be purchased online. ① *2–3 hr. See p 12,* **10**.

4 ★★ kids **Carousel on the Rose Fitzgerald Kennedy Greenway.** Just outside the doors of

The shark and ray touch tank at the New England Aquarium gives visitors a close encounter with the aquatic world.

the Aquarium is this appealing park, a block wide and 1½ miles long. At its the northern end is Greenway Carousel, located in the section called The Tiffany & Co. Foundation Grove. Instead of horses, the creatures on the ride include a lobster, a grasshopper, a peregrine falcon, and a harbor seal. The Carousel is designed to be accessible to individuals with physical, cognitive, and sensory disabilities. Nearby on the Greenway, the popular **Rings Fountain** is a spray fountain with rising jets that anyone can run through (kids often wear bathing suits here), and the **Harbor Fog Sculpture** emits a cool mist and sounds of the harbor in response to people moving through it. ◷ *1 hr. Carousel tickets $3. See p 11,* ⑨.

⑤ At last count there were 51 restaurant and food court options at the **Faneuil Hall Marketplace and Quincy Market** complex just steps from the Greenway. Sit-down options include Quincy's Place, an ice cream shop and sandwich cafe, and Wagamama, an Asian noodle restaurant. Food court options include mmMac n' Cheese, Regina Pizzeria, and Kilvert & Forbes Bakeshop. There are tables in the central atrium and benches outdoors. Public restrooms are available here. Food trucks also set up on the cross streets of the Greenway, with different options daily. *See p 9,* ②, *& www.rosekennedygreenway.org/visit/food.*

⑥ ★★★ kids **Boston Duck Tours.** The best motorized tour of Boston gives travelers a vantage point high above the street in a reconditioned World War II amphibious vehicle. The "Duck Boat" trundles around the city streets before slipping into the placid waters of the Charles River basin for a cruise of about 20 minutes. Con-duck-tors (ouch) are well trained—they need licenses to operate the mammoth vehicles on both land and water, and they spin off historical highlights with ease.

Samuel Adams spoke frequently at Faneuil Hall.

It's a pricey ticket, but also a unique combination of unusual perspectives and cooling breezes. Other water options include **ocean whale watch tours** (p 95, ❶) and **renting a canoe or kayak** on the Charles River (p 93, ❹). **Old Town Trolley** (☎ 855/396-7433; www.trolleytours. com) is another tour option that can shuttle you around town easily—guests can hop on and off trolleys all day long. ⏲ *80 min. Departure points at the New England Aquarium, Museum of Science, or Prudential Center. ☎ 617/267-3825. www.bostonducktours.com. Tickets $42 adults and kids 12 and older, $34 seniors, $28 kids 3–11, $11 kids 2 and under. Discounts available online. All tickets are for a specific time. Check ahead for schedules. In operation mid-Mar to late Nov daily 9am to 1 hr. before sunset. No tours Dec to mid-Mar. T: New England Aquarium, Museum of Science, or Prudential depending on departure point.*

❼ ★★★ **Museum of Science.** Many consider this the best indoor family destination in the Boston area. There are sections that focus on the moon, dinosaurs, the human body, and nanotechnology. Be sure to check the website in advance to sketch out a game plan for what to visit first. Also check in advance for the schedules for the on-premises **butterfly garden, IMAX theater,** and **planetarium,** which all have additional fees and tickets. The space is enormous and the trip can be overwhelming, with so many options—hands-on activities and experiments, interactive displays, and fascinating demonstrations—but it's both educational and entertaining, and there are sections for children of literally every age. The **Discovery Center** is like a quieter museum-within-a-museum, designed for the youngest visitors and kept at a limited capacity. Unlike most museums in Boston, this one has its own attached parking lot ($10–$22, depending on length of stay). Food options include burgers, burritos, pizza, a salad bar, and Starbucks. ⏲ *3–5 hr. 1 Science Park. ☎ 617/723-2500. www.mos.org. Museum admission $25 adults, $20 kids 3–11, free for kids 2 & under. Extra fees for butterfly garden, IMAX theater & planetarium, with discounted combination tickets available. Sat–Thurs 9am–5pm, Fri 9am–9pm; extended hours in summer & during school vacation;*

When Your Kid Needs to Run

If you're traveling with young children, you know that sometimes they just need open space to run or a good playground to spend an hour or two to. In addition to the **Boston Children's Museum** ❶, which is as much a three-story playground as it is a museum, and the **Rose Kennedy Greenway** ❹, which has expanses of nice grass, there's also small playground at the harbor in **Christopher Columbus Park** (p 11, ❽) and a medium-sized playground on the northern end of the **Boston Common** (p 33, ⓭). If you have a car, there's an expansive playground (and big parking lot) along the Charles River in Boston's Allston neighborhood that includes a popular **spray park and wading pool** in summer (p 93, ❹).

Boston Duck Tours' amphibious vehicles travel on both land and water.

theater & planetarium close later. T: Science Park.

8 ★★ kids **Harvard Museum of Natural History.** Dinosaurs, a giant hall of taxidermy, and glittery rocks and minerals makes this modest-sized museum in Cambridge's Harvard Square an appealing destination. ① 2–3 hr. See p 24, **4**.

9 **Food trucks** are set up daily (even in winter) at the Harvard Plaza just north of Harvard Yard, a 4-minute walk down Oxford Street from the Harvard Museum of Natural History. There are generally 4 or 5 options, which are likely to include something for picky eaters. The schedule is posted at www. commonspaces. harvard.edu/food-truck-schedule. Seating is available at outdoor tables and benches.

10 ★★★ kids **Tour of Fenway Park.** Fenway is the oldest and arguably most beloved venue in major league baseball—but you can't truly understand what the fuss is about until you see for yourself. A variety of daily tours run year-round and most include a trip to the stands, the press box, and the luxury seats. Some tours allow visitors to walk the warning track and touched the famed "Green Monster," the left-field wall, nicknamed for both its color and its 37.2 feet (11.3 m) height, which turns a lot of would-be home runs into doubles. See p 18, **12**, for more about Fenway. ① 15 min.–1 hr., depending on tour. 4 Jersey St. (formerly Yawkey Way). www.mlb.com/app/ballpark/redsox/ballpark/tours. Tickets can be purchased online up to 30 days in advance; a limited number of same-day tickets are available on a first-come, first-served basis at Fenway's Gate D. Tours $14–$50. Daily 9am–5pm or 3 hr. before game time on game days. T: Kenmore.

11 The accurately named **Tasty Burger**—first established in this location, in a renovated service station—also serves hot dogs and chicken sandwiches. It's the Official Burger of the Boston Red Sox and it's available here and inside the ballpark. 1301 Boylston St. ☎ 617/425-4444. www.tastyburger.com. $.

A full-size model of a Tyrannosaurus rex greets visitors at the Museum of Science.

Discount Tickets: Practical Matters

CityPass (☎ 888/330-5008; www.citypass.com/boston) is a booklet of tickets providing discount admission to **New England Aquarium, Museum of Science, Prudential Skywalk Observatory,** and **Harvard Museum of Natural History** or **Boston Harbor Cruises.** If you visit five attractions, the price ($59 for individuals 12 and older, $47 for youths 3–11) provides a discount of nearly 50% on buying tickets individually. Passes are good for 9 consecutive days from date of purchase. They're on sale at participating attractions or online. Tickets in hand means you can skip ticket lines, too.

⓬ ★★★ **kids Museum of Fine Arts.** The MFA provides special programming for kids and families, including twice-monthly 45-minute "playdates" for ages 2 to 4 and two-hour in-gallery drawing for kids ages 5 to 8 every Saturday morning (and for anybody every Wednesday from 5 to 9pm). Family activity tote bags with self-guided tour-activity sheets, a sketchpad, and colored pencils are available for free at the Sharf Visitor Center.

Fenway Park, the oldest major league baseball stadium in the U.S., is located right in Boston.

An audio/video mobile tour specially designed for children 6 to 10 is available for $4 (see www.mfa.org/visit/mfa-guide/kids). ⓢ *1–3 hr. See p 22,* ❶.

⓭ ★★ **Boston Common and Boston Public Garden.** The Common has a playground, Carousel, and Frog Pond (spray pool in summer, ice skating rink in winter, and reflecting pool the rest of the time). The adjacent Garden offers well-kept lawns, *Make way for Ducklings* statues, and snoozy Swan Boat rides. ⓢ *1–2 hr. See p 88.*

⓮ A small Boston-based chain with 7 locations in the city, **Boloco** is the go-to for fast, tasty, and healthy burritos and bowls, and the occasional fun specials, such as the cheeseburger burrito (really). To the right of the front door, at the corner of Boylston and Charles streets, look for the statue of Edgar Allen Poe and The Raven bursting from his carrying case and erected here in 2014. Poe was born in Boston and grew to loathe it—but no matter, Boston is still happy to claim the connection. *176 Boylston St. See p 103.*

Boston's Freedom Trail

1 Boston Common
2 Robert Gould Shaw Memorial and the 54th Massachusetts Regiment Memorial
3 Massachusetts State House
4 Park Street Church
5 Granary Burying Ground
6 King's Chapel & Burying Ground
7 Benjamin Franklin Statue
8 Old Corner Bookstore Building
9 Old South Meeting House
10 Old State House
11 Site of the Boston Massacre
12 Faneuil Hall, Faneuil Hall Marketplace, and Quincy Market
13' Durgin Park
14 The New England Holocaust Memorial
15 Paul Revere House
16' Artu
17 James Rego Square (Paul Revere Mall)
18 Old North Church (Christ Church)
19 Copp's Hill Burying Ground and Copp's Hill Terrace
20 USS Constitution
21 USS Constitution Museum
22 Bunker Hill Monument

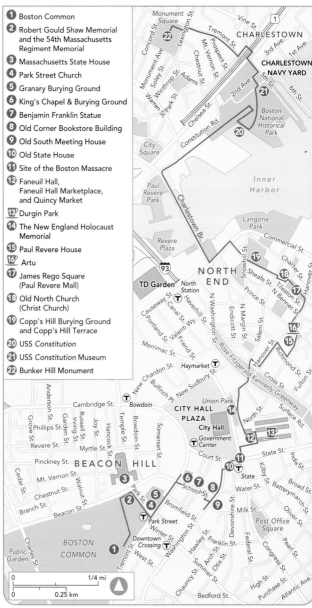

The Freedom Trail is a walking path that winds through 2½ miles of historic Boston. The trail passes 16 sites from the 17th, 18th, and 19th centuries, all listed here, plus a few others, including places to eat. The Freedom Trail has a website, www.thefreedomtrail.org, and a Twitter feed, @thefreedomtrail. If you follow the full route, give yourself 4 hours to allow for walking, reading plaques and lingering, and a serendipitous detour or two. This itinerary follows the usual order of the red-lined route. START: **T to Park Street.**

❶ ★★ **Boston Common.** The oldest public park in the country (founded in 1634), the Common is a welcome splash of green in red-brick Boston. The park **visitor center** (139 Tremont St.) is next to the fountain. **Freedom Trail tours with costumed guides** ($12 adults, $6.50 kids 6–12) start here and last 90 minutes; see www.thefreedomtrail.org/book-tour/public-tours.shtml. For information about this prominent city park, see p 88. ⏱ *10 min. Bordered by Park, Tremont, Boylston, Charles, and Beacon sts. Free admission. Daily 24 hr. T: Park Street.*

❷ ★★★ **Robert Gould Shaw and the 54th Massachusetts Regiment Memorial.** At the highest point of the Common, up the hill and near to the State House, is a magnificent bronze sculpture. It honors the first American army unit comprised of free black soldiers, the Union Army's 54th Massachusetts Colored Regiment, which fought in the Civil War under the command of Col. Robert Gould Shaw (1837–1863). The plaque on the back provides rich historical detail. The incredible artistry of Augustus Saint-Gaudens' relief took 14 years to design and execute. The story of Shaw and the 54th Regiment was told in the 1989 movie "Glory." ⏱ *10 min. Beacon St. at Park St. Free admission. Daily 24 hr. T: Park Street.*

Freedom Trail marker.

❸ ★ **Massachusetts State House.** The gracious golden-dome-topped state capitol is a signature work of the great Federal-era architect Charles Bulfinch. Note the symmetry, a hallmark of Federal style, in details as large as doors and as small as moldings. Visitors can take self-guided tours (see www.sec.state.ma.us/trs/trsbok/trstour.htm) or, by prior arrangement, guided tours. Allow time to investigate the statues and monuments that dot the grounds, including **President John F. Kennedy captured in mid-stride.** The 60-foot-tall eagle-topped column at the back of the building (at Bowdoin St.) represents the original height of Beacon Hill before it was cut down to fill 19th-century landfill projects. ⏱ *20 min. to explore outside; 45 min. with guided tour. 24 Beacon St.* ☎ *617/727-3676. www.sec.state.ma.us/trs/trsgen/genidx.htm. Free admission and tours. Mon–Fri 8:45am–5pm (tours 10am–3:30pm). T: Park St.*

4 Park Street Church. Most Bostonians know this redbrick church for its 217-foot clock tower and steeple, which chimes on the quarter-hour. "My Country 'Tis of Thee" was sung on the church's steps for the first time on July 4, 1831. This is an active church, with Sunday services. ⏱ *10 min. 1 Park St.* ☎ *617/523-3383. www.park street.org. July–Aug Tues–Sat & Sun year-round. T: Park St.*

5 ★★ kids Granary Burying Ground. Colonial Boston's residents clustered in what's now the downtown area, working, worshipping, and burying their dead here. Established in 1660, this cemetery got its name from the granary, or grain-storage building, that once stood on the site of Park Street Church **4**. Wander the walkways to take in the diversity of markers and ornamental carvings, including the "Soul Effigy," a skull or "death's head" with wings on each side. The map near the entrance shows the locations of the graves of Crispus Attucks and other victims of the Boston Massacre, Paul Revere, Samuel Adams, and John Hancock, whose monument is almost as florid as his signature. Also here: Elizabeth "Mother" Goose, who may or may not be "the" Mother Goose of nursery rhyme fame. ⏱ *15 min. Tremont St. at Bromfield St. Free admission. Daily 10am–5pm. T Park St.*

6 ★★ King's Chapel and Burying Ground. King's Chapel was established as an Anglican church in 1686, and it became

Paul Revere's grave in Granary Burying Ground.

Unitarian after the Revolution. The current chapel (1749) is the country's oldest church in continuous use as well as its oldest major stone building. Designed by the architect of Christ Church in Cambridge, the granite building was built around its wooden predecessor, which was then removed (and rebuilt in Nova Scotia). The small graveyard alongside it dates to 1630, the same year Europeans settled the peninsula. Buried here are Mary Chilton, the first woman to come ashore in Plymouth in 1620, Elizabeth Pain, reputedly the model for Hester Prynne in *The Scarlet Letter*, and John Winthrop, the first colonial governor. This is an active church, and it hosts **lunchtime concerts on Tuesdays** (p 126). ⏱ *15 min. 58 Tremont St.* ☎ *617/523-1749. www. kings-chapel.org. Donation $3 suggested. Chapel year-round Mon–Sat from 10am, Sun from 1:30pm; check website for closing time. Tours several times a day; check website. Burying ground daily 9am–5pm, with shorter hours in winter. T: Government Center.*

7 Benjamin Franklin Statue. The 1856 statue of Benjamin

Franklin—publisher, statesman, postmaster, scientist—sits behind the fence that surrounds the ornate **Old City Hall,** the seat of Boston government until 1969. Franklin was born a block away, and this is the city's first portrait statue. The colorful sidewalk mosaic out front marks the original site of the first public school in the United States, Boston Latin. ① *5 min. 45 School St.*

❽ Old Corner Bookstore Building. This land once belonged to religious reformer Anne Hutchinson, who was excommunicated and banished from Massachusetts for heresy in 1638. The structure here, which today has a Chipotle restaurant on the ground floor, dates to 1718 (which makes it 300 years old in 2018). In the mid-1800s the building was the center of U.S. publishing and home of publisher Ticknor & Fields whose authors included Harriet Beecher Stowe, Oliver Wendell Holmes Sr., and Louisa May Alcott. Step across the street to appreciate the scale and the very existence of this building, which was already old when the American Revolution was just breaking out. Across the street is the **Irish Famine Memorial.** ① *5 min. 283 Washington St.*

❾ ★ kids Old South Meeting House. The Boston Tea Party, one of the pivotal political demonstrations of the pre-Revolutionary era, started here in 1773. The displays and exhibits in the former house of worship—now used for lectures, concerts, and other events—tell the story in a low-key yet compelling fashion. ① *15 min. 310 Washington St.* ☎ *617/482-6439. www.osmh. org. Admission $6 adults, $5 seniors & students, $1 kids 5–17, free for kids 4 & under. Daily 9:30am–5pm; shorter hours in winter. T: State.*

❿ ★★ kids Old State House. Like a William Morris flower in a forest of skyscrapers, this fancy little brick building sits amid towering neighbors. On the exterior are vestigial traces of British rule—a lion and a unicorn, both royal symbols that predate the Revolution—and in fact the State House opened in 1713, when Massachusetts was a British colony and State Street was named King Street. (In the 1630s, when the Puritan settlement was in its infancy, the whipping post and stocks awaited sinners on this site.) In 1776, the Declaration of Independence was first read to Bostonians from the balcony. The building served as the state capitol from Revolutionary times until the present State House ❸ opened in 1798. Today it houses a history museum, including photographs, maps, John Hancock's coat, and a sound and light presentation about the Boston Massacre ⓫. Tours are included with admission. ① *30 min. 206 Washington St.* ☎ *617/720-1713. www.boston history.org. Admission $10 adults, $8.50 seniors and students, free for kids 18 and under. Daily 9am–5pm (until 6pm May–early Sept). T: State.*

The Declaration of Independence was read from the Old State House balcony in 1776.

⓫ Site of the Boston Massacre. A circle of cobblestones underneath the Old State House balcony honors the five men killed by British troops on March 5, 1770. The event fueled the already simmering discontent with British authority, and Paul Revere created an engraved image that helped publicize the incident and galvanize rebellion. ⏱ *5 min. Intersection of State, Devonshire & Congress sts.*

⓬ ★★ kids Faneuil Hall, Faneuil Hall Marketplace, and Quincy Market. The front building, Faneuil Hall, dates to 1742 as a meeting house and site of political activism. The commercial complex behind it—Faneuil Hall Marketplace and Quincy Market—is housed in restored 19th-century buildings and is a popular tourist attraction. ⏱ *45 min. See p 9,* ❶ *and* ❷.

⓭ Part authentic historic eatery, part show, **Durgin-Park** is still a trusty and upbeat venue for Boston classics—clam chowder, baked beans, and broiled scrod among them. *340 Faneuil Hall Marketplace. See p 104.*

Millions of numbers are etched into the Holocaust Memorial's six glass towers, honoring those killed.

⓮ ★★ kids The New England Holocaust Memorial. Dedicated in 1995, this outdoor memorial, designed by Stanley Saitowitz, comprises six glass towers, each 54 feet tall and lit internally. Millions of numbers are etched in the glass, representing the numerical tattoos etched into Holocaust victims' arms. The memorial isn't formally on the Freedom Trail, but is a fitting addition to this tour. ⏱ *15 min. Union St. (North & Hanover sts.)* ☎ *617/457-8755. www.nehm.org. T: Haymarket.*

⓯ ★★★ kids Paul Revere House. Built about 1680 and now a national historic landmark, this home is one of the few surviving dwellings of its age in the United States. Revere was a talented silversmith who supported a large family—his first wife, Sarah, died after giving birth to their 8th child, and his second wife, Rachel, also bore 8 children. When the family moved in in 1770, there were 3 adults—Revere, Sarah, and his mother Deborah—and the first 5 children. Revere owned the house for another 30 years. ⏱ *30 min. 19 North Sq. See p 10,* ❼.

⓰ **Artú** is right on the Freedom Trail and a good option for pastas, paninis, and pizzas. *6 Prince St. See p 102.*

⓱ ★★ James Rego Square (Paul Revere Mall). This narrow, tree-lined, brick-laid plaza is the site of one of the most iconic and photographed tableaus of Boston: the statue of Paul Revere atop a horse, with the Old North Church ⓲ behind him. ⏱ *10 min. Off Hanover St., at Clark St.*

⓲ ★★★ kids Old North Church (Christ Church). This beautifully proportioned brick church, designed in the style of Sir

Christopher Wren, overflows with historic associations. It contains the oldest American church bells, the Revere family's pew, and a bust of George Washington that's believed to be the first memorial to the first president. It was here that sexton Robert Newman briefly hung two lanterns in the steeple on the night of April 18, 1775, signaling to the rebellious colonists that British troops were leaving Boston by water ("two if by sea"), bound for Lexington and Concord. Somehow, through nearly 300 years of rough New England weather, the original weather vane has survived atop the 191-ft steeple—the tallest in Boston. Tours takes visitors up into the spire and down to the crypt—not for the claustrophobic. There are tranquil gardens on the north side of the building. ⓒ *40 min. 193 Salem St. See p 10,* ⑥.

The Old North Church, the oldest church building in Boston, dates to 1723.

⓳ ★ Copp's Hill Burying Ground and Copp's Hill Terrace.

The highest point in the North End affords a panoramic view across the Inner Harbor to the wishbone-shaped Zakim Bunker Hill Memorial Bridge and the Charlestown Navy Yard, where the three masts of **USS *Constitution*** ⓴ poke into view. (The British set their cannons here to fire at Charlestown during the Battle of Bunker Hill in 1775.) Boston's first African-American neighborhood was nearby, and an estimated 1,000 of the 10,000 or so people buried in the graveyard at the crest of Copp's Hill were black. The best known is Prince Hall, who is believed to have fought at Bunker Hill and later founded the first black Masonic lodge. Author Phillis Wheatley is believed to lie in an unmarked grave here. Also here is the family plot of prominent Puritan ministers Increase Mather (who was also president of Harvard) and

Cotton Mather (Increase's son). To get to Copp's Hill Terrace, a small park lower on the hill designed by Frederick Law Olmsted, you'll need exit the burying ground the way you entered and walk down Hull Street, around Snow Hill Street, then up Charter Street. ⓒ *20 min. Burying Ground: Hull St., at Snowhill St. Daily 10am–5pm. Terrace: Charter St. at Snowhill St. Daily 24 hr. T: North Station.*

⓴ ★★ kids USS *Constitution.*

Built just a few blocks from Copp's Hill and launched in 1797, this exceptional tall ship is the oldest commissioned floating warship in the world. ⓒ *1 hr., including security screening. Charlestown Navy Yard. See p 47,* ❶.

㉑ ★ kids Bunker Hill Monument.

Visitors with the energy to climb the 294 steps of this granite obelisk are rewarded with expansive views of Boston and the harbor. ⓒ *20 min. if you stay on the ground and visit the museum; 1 hr. if you climb the stairs. See p 49,* ❺.

Architecture of Copley Square

1 Trinity Church
2 John Hancock Tower
3 The Fairmont Copley Plaza
4 Oak Long Bar + Kitchen
5 Boston Public Library
6 Eataly
7 Old South Church
8 Trinity Church Rectory
9 Former Boston Museum of Natural History
10 Church of the Covenant
11 Emmanuel Church
12 Arlington Street Church

Copley Square is the heart of commercial Boston. Landmark buildings occupy three sides of a lovely plaza, and a constant flow of pedestrians enlivens the area. Named for the celebrated artist John Singleton Copley (1738–1815), the area is a central locale for summer festivals, a farmers' market, and April's Boston Marathon, whose finish line is here and where the city experienced a brutal bombing in 2013. It's a visual treat year-round and the hub of the hub. START: **T to Copley.**

❶ ★★★ Trinity Church. One of the best-known church buildings in the country, Trinity Church is architect H. H. Richardson's masterwork (his style was so distinctive that it now bears his name: Richardsonian Romanesque). While the prototypical New England church is simple— white with a towering steeple— Trinity is anything but. Before you enter, take in the busy yet harmonious design of the polychrome (multicolored) exterior. The 1877 building is granite, trimmed with red sandstone, with a roof of red tiles. The 221-foot tower weighs 90 million pounds all on its own. Inside, barrel vaults draw the eye up to the 63-foot ceilings, and murals and decorative painting by John La Farge make imaginative use of colored plaster that complements the hues in the stained-glass windows (look for La Farge's window *Christ in Majesty*, in the west gallery). The structure rests on 4,502 pilings driven into the mud that was once the Back Bay, and the pilings must be kept wet so they don't rot. A tour is the best way to fully absorb the building's remarkable construction. Among the regular events presented here are **Choral Evensong** on Wednesdays at 5:45pm and an **Organ Recital Series** Fridays at 12:15pm. The church also hosts a variety of public events, including lectures and community outreach. ⏱ *1 hr. 206 Clarendon St.* ☎ *617/536-0944. www.trinitychurchboston.org. Free*

Trinity Church is the masterwork of architect H. H. Richardson.

admission & free tours following Sunday service. Guided or self-guided tour $7 adults, $5 seniors & students, free for children 15 & under. Organ concerts $10 suggested donation. Wed–Sat 10am–4:30pm, Sun 12:15pm–4:30pm. T: Copley.

❷ ★ John Hancock Tower. This reflecting-glass behemoth is remarkable for what it isn't—obtrusive, distracting, or incongruous. It somehow complements rather than competes with its neighbors, and provides wonderful reflections of Trinity Church. (It does also create a wind-tunnel effect for several blocks in all directions.) The office building—renamed 200 Clarendon in

2015 (though everyone stills calls it Hancock Tower)—is not open to the public, and the top-floor observation deck, once a popular attraction, closed in 2001. *200 Clarendon St.*

❸ ★ Fairmont Copley Plaza.

The relatively austere facade of the 1912 hotel conceals a wildly sumptuous interior that's well worth a look—be sure to check out the lobby ceiling. (*Bonus:* A black Labrador named Catie Copley hangs around in the lobby—hotel guests can schedule walks or runs with her—and you can probably pet her if she's there.) Architect Henry Janeway Hardenbergh, who had help on this project from local architect Clarence Blackall, also designed New York's Plaza Hotel and Dakota apartment building. *138 St. James Ave. See p 139.*

📷 The elegant **OAK Long Bar + Kitchen** inside Fairmont Copley Plaza serves swanky drinks and farm-to-table eats all day long. *In the Fairmont Copley Plaza Hotel. See p 117.*

In 2015, the official name of this icon of the Boston cityscape changed to "200 Clarendon," but most people still call it the Hancock Tower.

❺ ★★★ Boston Public Library.

The main branch of the city's library system is an active, modern public gathering space. A $78 million renovation completed in 2016 created an airy, light-filled front atrium complete with a large welcome center, the vibrant **Newsfeed Café,** loads of cafe-style seating, and an **open on-air radio studio** for WGBH, one of the city's two public radio powerhouses. A new colorful **children's library** doubled the space for kids. The library's calendar lists 5 to 10 events a day, including public lectures, book sales, classes in 3D modeling software, a Lego club, ESL conversation groups, Tinker Tots science activities for the 3-to-5 set, and free tours of the grand building's art and architecture. Overall, the changes are an architectural marvel and have brought a welcome energy to the public resource, which was built in 1895.

Architect Charles Follen McKim of the legendary New York firm of McKim, Mead & White gets the credit for the facility's initial design, but he was really the captain of an artistic all-star team. The library's bronze doors are the work of sculptor Daniel Chester French (who created the seated Abraham Lincoln at the presidential memorial in Washington, D.C., and the John Harvard statue in Cambridge), Augustus Saint-Gaudens created the decorative seals above each of the three entrance arches, and Pierre Puvis de Chavannes created the murals on the staircase and in the second-floor corridor, which represent the wisdom and knowledge collected in the building. On the third floor is the **Sargent Gallery,** which houses murals by John Singer Sargent illustrating religious themes. The celebrated portraitist worked on them from 1895 through 1916, and many visitors consider this gallery their

Inside Copley Square, the Park

The Copley Square plaza itself is a relatively small green park, crisscrossed by paths and with benches for relaxing. A **farmers market** sets up here Tuesdays and Fridays from mid-May through late November. **Festivals** also are centered here, including First Night celebrations on New Year's Eve and summer music concerts. A **BosTix Booth** for discount theater tickets is located on the northwest corner (p 131). A whimsical statue near Trinity Church of *The Tortoise & Hare* is a nod to the Boston Marathon, whose finish line is down the block in front of the Boston Public Library; it was created by Nancy Schön, who also sculpted *Make Way for Ducklings* in the Public Garden.

favorite part of the library. There's also an especially lovely **interior courtyard** designed in the manner of a Renaissance cloister, with a Roman arcade, fountain basin with water jets, and eternally peaceful atmosphere. Free guided tours are available daily, and the library has materials for self-guided tours on its website. The **Boston Marathon finish line** is directly outside the Boylston Street entrance and stays painted on the street year-round. ⏱ *1 hr. 700 Boylston St.* ☎ *617/ 536-5400. www.bpl.org. Mon–Thurs 9am–9pm, Fri–Sat 9am–5pm, Sun 1–5pm. 1-hour guided Art &*

Architecture Tours free. See www. bpl.org/central/tours.htm for schedule & to download materials for self-guided tours. T: Copley.

If the appealing **Newsfeed Café** (www.thecateredaffair.com/bpl/ newsfeed-cafe) inside the front entrance of the Boston Public Library is too busy, head down the block to 🟦6 **Eataly** for more options. The 3-story Italian emporium has 4 restaurants and eight take-out counters including gelato, panini, focaccia and pizza, and rotisserie foods. *800 Boylston St.* ☎ *617/236-5800. $–$$.*

The main staircase of the Boston Public Library features marble twin lions.

IN HONOR
OF THE
~~~SACHUSETTS~~ VOLUNTEER INFANTRY

7 ★ Old South Church. This Northern Italian Gothic structure anchors its corner of Copley Square with authority. Now with an active parish of the United Church of Christ, the building itself was constructed from 1872 through 1875. The multicolored facade (the technical term for the design on the entrance arches is *zebra-striped*) encloses a similarly vivid sanctuary, illuminated with stained glass throughout. The Gothic influence is particularly evident in the chapel, to the left as you enter, and the design of the windows. ⏲ *10 min.* 645 Boylston St. ☎ 617/536-1970. www.oldsouth.org. Mon–Fri 8am–7pm, Sat 10am–4pm, Sun 8:30am–7pm. T: Copley.

8 Trinity Church Rectory. H. H. Richardson designed this rectory, which was completed in 1879, 2 years after the church (p 41, **1**). The style is considered Richardsonian Romanesque, but this building is considerably less elaborate than the landmark house of worship. It is now office space for the church. *233 Clarendon St.*

Old South Church.

Newbury Street is lined with outdoor cafes.

9 ★ Former Boston Museum of Natural History. Pop in just to gawk: The opulent 1863 building, a graceful French Academic design by William Preston, now houses a Restoration Hardware store. But what a grand space it is! *Architectural Digest* noted when "RH Boston" opened in 2013 that the building has "graceful Corinthian pilasters, Romanesque arches, and a monumental interior atrium," a "gilded, coffered ceiling," and the "pièce de résistance: a glass elevator modeled after the one in Los Angeles's 1893 Bradbury Building." ⏲ *10 min.* 234 Berkeley St.

10 ★ Church of the Covenant. Tiffany Glass and Decorating Company produced the 42 stained glass windows here, including the well-known Sparrow Window, which depicts Jesus as carpenter. All can be previewed on the church's website. ⏲ *20 min.* 67 Newbury St. ☎ 617/266-7480. cotcbos.org. Mon, Wed–Sat 11am–3pm, Sun 12:30–4:30pm. By appointment only in winter. T: Arlington.

11 ★ Emmanuel Church. The main part of this church was the first building completed on Newbury Street, in 1862. The Gothic

Maintaining Facilities *and* Missions

Sustaining important, historic churches is not an easy task. Emmanuel Church explains the dilemma—and its own steps toward a solution—eloquently on its website: "As is often the case with urban churches, Emmanuel Church was built for a large and affluent congregation, which migrated to the suburbs during the mid-twentieth century, leaving a small congregation responsible for a large, historic, and expensive edifice. Emmanuel Church views its building as a resource, not only for itself, but for the larger community of the city of Boston, and has found that by careful management and partnership with a wide variety of programs and institutions we have been able to maintain our historic building while supporting our missions of Social Justice and the Arts. Although in a typical week the congregation of Emmanuel Episcopal Church holds only one worship service, on the building calendar one finds between 30 and 40 events of many different types, run by many different organizations, and in addition it provides a home for a women's shelter, an outreach program for homeless men, two resident artists, and, of course, offices for Emmanuel Church, Emmanuel Music, and Central Reform Temple."

Revival exterior unites three separate spaces; the loveliest is the **Leslie Lindsey Memorial Chapel,** named for a Bostonian who died on her honeymoon in 1915 when a German U-boat torpedoed the *Lusitania.* She died wearing the diamonds and rubies her father had given her as a wedding gift, and her parents sold the jewels to finance the construction of the chapel. The stained-glass window representing St. Cecilia was modeled on the young bride. From September through May, the 10am **Sunday services include Bach cantatas** performed live by the outstanding orchestra and chorus of **Emmanuel Music** (p 125). ◷ *10 min. 15 Newbury St.* ☎ *617/536-3355. www. emmanuelboston.org. T: Arlington.*

⓬ ★ **Arlington Street Church.** Directly on the Boston Public Garden and constructed from 1859 to 1861 (although its congregation

dates to 1729), this was the first building completed in Back Bay. Architect Arthur Gilman designed the exterior to resemble the Church of St. Martin-in-the-Fields in London's Trafalgar Square. The Italianate interior is famous for the stained-glass windows designed by Louis Comfort Tiffany between 1899 and 1929—they're considered some of the artist's finest work. The church's **Arlington Street Church Tiffany Education Center** (www. asctiffany.org) has an online tour with audio. In-person self-guided tours (follow audio on your smartphone) as well as docent-guided tours are available on a limited basis. ◷ *30 min. 351 Boylston St.* ☎ *617/536-7050. www.ascboston. org. Check www.asctiffany.org/visit for tour schedule & open hours for visiting. Suggested donation of $5 for tours. T: Arlington.*

Charlestown's Naval Heritage

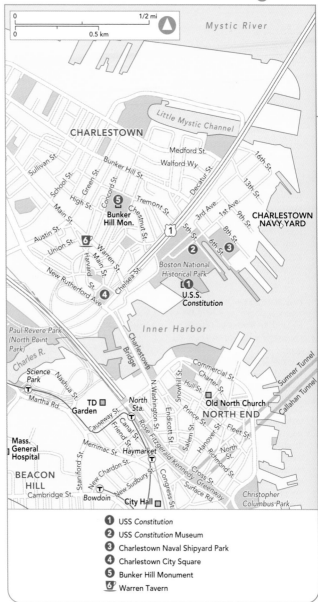

1. USS *Constitution*
2. USS *Constitution* Museum
3. Charlestown Naval Shipyard Park
4. Charlestown City Square
5. Bunker Hill Monument
6. Warren Tavern

Charlestown is a waterfront neighborhood of Boston located across the Inner Harbor from the North End. It's home to the USS *Constitution* and the Charlestown Naval yard, and site of the Bunker Hill Monument, a granite obelisk that overlooks Boston from afar. Charlestown was originally settled as its own entity in 1629 (a year before Boston proper), but became part of the city in 1874. It retains an air of individuality and has a new sheen of gentrification. START: **T to North Station plus a 20 min. walk over the Charlestown Bridge, or ferry from Long Wharf (Aquarium T stop) to Charlestown Navy Yard. See p 161 for ferry information.**

❶ ★★ kids USS *Constitution*.

This magnificent frigate's three masts loom over the navy yard, and its rich black hull is one of the most eye-catching sights on the harbor. Built in a Boston shipyard at what's now 409 Commercial Street and launched in 1797, the 204-foot-long ship is the oldest commissioned floating warship in the world. It earned its nickname "Old Ironsides" on August 19, 1812, when, during an engagement with HMS *Guerriere* in the War of 1812, cannonballs bounced off its thick oak hull as if it were metal. Old Ironsides never lost a battle, but narrowly escaped destruction several times in its first 2 centuries. Today the *Constitution* is a museum ship and an active-duty posting for the sailors who lead the tours (wearing replica post-war 1813 uniforms), and a beloved symbol of Boston. After being dry-docked for a 2-year renovation, the ship was returned to her pier in July 2017. The tour provides a fascinating overview as well as a great opportunity to mingle with people from all over the country and around the world. ⏱ *1 hr., including security screening. 1 Constitution Road, Charlestown Navy Yard.* ☎ *617/242-7511. www. nps.gov/bost/learn/historyculture/ ussconst.htm & www.navy.mil/local/ constitution & www.navy.mil/ah_ online/constitution/index.html. Free admission. Visitors 18 & older & must present a valid federal or state issued*

The USS Constitution, *commissioned in 1797, got the nickname "Old Ironsides" after cannonballs bounced off its oak hull.*

photo ID or passport at the ship's security entrance. Wed–Sun 10am–4pm; check website. Free tours year-round every 30 min. T: North Station & 20-min. walk or ferry from Long Wharf.

❷ ★ kids USS *Constitution* Museum.

The *Constitution* is mostly a hands-off experience, but this engaging museum is exactly the opposite. Visitors pull ropes, push buttons, construct simple

Quincy Market architect Alexander Parris also designed the USS Constitution Museum building.

model ships, practice holystoning (scrubbing) the deck, and play dress-up. The granite building was originally the navy yard's wood and metal shop. While the ship itself is not wheelchair accessible, the museum is. ⏱ *30 min. Charlestown Navy Yard, Building 22.* ☎ *617/426-1812. www.ussconstitutionmuseum. org. Suggested donation $5–$10 adults, $3–$5 kids, $20–$25 families. Apr–Oct daily 9am–6pm; Nov–Mar 10am–5pm. T: Ferry from Long Wharf, or North Station & 20-min. walk.*

❸ ★ **Charlestown Naval Shipyard Park.** If you come to Charlestown via the Boston Harbor water shuttle (10-min., $3.50; p 163), you'll land here at the 30-acre Boston National Historical Park. The streets and docks that surround it were a shipyard that built, supplied, and maintained U.S. Navy vessels from 1800 to 1974. At its height, during World War II, the facility employed more than 40,000 people—including sizeable numbers of women (some 15–20% of the workers), who filled in for men who had been shipped out. Although it's no longer an active base, it's home to the USS *Constitution* and has been

repurposed for residential, office, and lab space. There are military monuments and explanatory plaques galore. ⏱ *15 min. The Navy Yard Visitor Center is in Building 5 (near USS Constitution) through Gate 1, by pedestrian access only. All center visitors must first enter through the security screening building & present a valid federal- or state-issued photo ID or passport.* ☎ *617/242-5601. https://go.nps. gov/cny. Grounds open 24 hr.; visitor center Tues–Sun 9am–5pm. Free admission. T: Ferry from Long Wharf, or North Station & 20-min. walk.*

❹ ★ **Charlestown City Square.** Until the 1980s, this was a grim patch of asphalt beneath a thundering highway overpass. Today it's one of the most pleasant side effects of the Big Dig, the highway-construction project that took over Boston in the 1990s and moved the highway underground. Opened in 1996, the park is a 1-acre oasis of lawns, trees, shrubs, flowers, and benches, dotted with plaques, memorials, and a fountain. Sculptures include a crane at the top of the fountain (the Three Cranes Tavern once stood on this site) and numerous cod, honoring the integral role the fish once played in Boston's economy. *Rutherford Ave. & Chelsea St. www.boston.gov/neighborhood/charlestown.*

5 ★ **kids Bunker Hill Monument.** The narrow pedestrian streets of Charlestown all seem to lead to this elegant square. The 221-foot granite obelisk at the center, designed by the prolific Solomon Willard, commemorates the Battle of Bunker Hill on June 17, 1775 (June 17 is now Bunker Hill Day, a holiday in Massachusetts' Suffolk County). The British won that battle, but nearly half of their troops were killed or wounded. Partly as a consequence of the carnage, royal forces abandoned Boston 9 months later. The exhibits in the small but engaging **Battle of Bunker Hill Museum** across the street from the grass lawn (43 Monument Square) tell the story of the fire fight (be sure to get to the second floor, for the 360-degree painting depicting the combat). **Bunker Hill Lodge** adjoins the Monument and houses artwork and a Revolutionary War cannon; this is where you enter if you want to climb up. Think hard before attempting to walk the 294 stairs to the top; it's a tough climb that ends at a small space with tiny windows. ⏱ *20 min. if you stay on the ground & visit the museum; 1 hr. if you climb the stairs. Monument Sq. at Monument Ave.* ☎ *617/242-7275. www.nps.gov/bost/planyourvisit/bhm.htm. Free admission to the monument & museum. Monument & museum daily 9am–5pm in summer & 1–5pm rest of the year. T: Community College.*

6 Even if you don't eat here, at least step in for a look: **Warren Tavern** was built around 1780 after the British torched Charlestown as they withdrew in 1775, destroying most of its pre-Revolutionary buildings. The Tavern is pleasant and often busy with both tourists and locals. It's open daily for lunch and dinner. *2 Pleasant St.* ☎ *617/241-8142. www.warrentavern.com. $–$$.*

Next to the Bunker Hill Monument is a statue of William Prescott, who gave the legendary command: "Don't fire until you see the whites of their eyes."

Romantic Boston

1 Be an evening guest at the Gardiner Museum
2 Ice skate hand in hand on the Boston Common
3 Steal away for weekend brunch in the South End
4 Sail the seas on the Boston Harbor Water Shuttle
5 Splurge for a special meal at L'Espalier
6 Indulge in a spa treatment at G2O Spa & Salon
7 Amble through the Boston Public Garden
8 Take in a concert at Jordan Hall
9 Poke along Charles Street and the winding streets off it
10 Check into the Eliot Hotel
11 Have a drink at Top of the Hub Jazz Lounge
12 Dance under the stars at the ICA

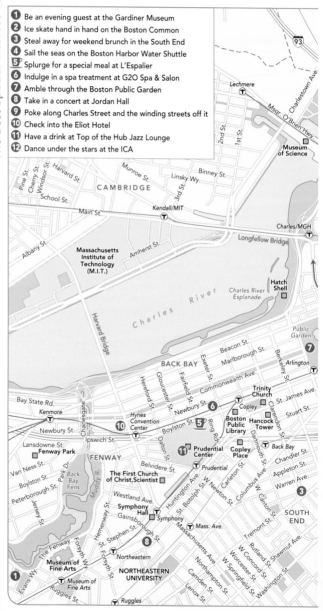

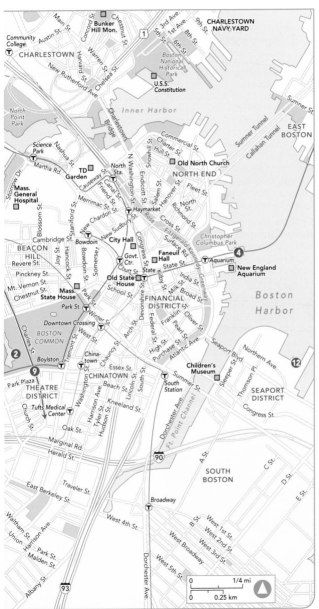

Romance is in the eye of the beholder, and what one person finds appealing another may find a snooze. With that caveat in mind, consider the list below a sampling of some of the most appealing options for evocative, dreamy moments—from the simple to the extravagant.

❶ Be an evening guest at the Gardner Museum. If you happen to be in town for the monthly Third Thursdays at Gardner, stroll the galleries and perch next to the lavish courtyard garden with wine and music—for a few hours, this Venetian-style palazzo is your own play area. The museum's urbane Café G is also open for snacks and dinner. ○ *2–3 hr. Third Thursday runs from 5–9pm. See p 23,* ❸.

❷ Skate hand-in-hand on the Boston Common. Frog Pond becomes a picture-perfect outdoor ice skating rink in winter, with teeny lights decorating the surrounding trees. Afterwards, a trip to nearby L. A. Burdick Chocolate Shop is the place to indulge in hot chocolate and a sumptuous pastry. ○ *2 hr. See p 33,* ⓭, *& p 91,* ❾.

Union Park, in the South End, dates from the late 1850s and is surrounded by brick row houses.

❸ Steal away for weekend brunch in the South End. Aquitaine Bar á Vin Bistrot serves up a large menu of brunch items on weekends 9am to 3pm—options include omelette Alsacienne, shrimp & grits, and malted Belgian waffle—with an elegant, French atmosphere to accompany it. Stroll afterwards to Union Park, a block away. A 1-block stretch of brick row houses surrounds a small oval park and makes for one of the prettiest settings in the city. The lawn (for looking only) has trees, flowers, and two bubbling fountains. ○ *2–3 hr. See p 102.*

❹ Sail the seas on the Boston Harbor Water Shuttle. Getting out on the water is the best part of any cruise, but riding the 10-min. ferry to Charlestown and back costs far less than a formal tour ($3.50 each way) and gives you more control of your schedule. The ferry lands you in Charlestown Naval Shipyard Park, a 30-acre (12 hectare) Boston National Historical Park. ○ *1 hr. See p 48,* ❸.

❺ Splurge for a special meal at L'Espalier. If you or the person you want to impress is of the school that special meals should include caviar, truffles, and a cheese course before dessert, put L'Espalier—the city's premier white-tablecloth restaurant—at the top of your culinary bucket list. ○ *2–3 hr. See p 106.*

❻ Indulge in a spa treatment at G2O Spa & Salon. Treat yourself, a friend, or both of you to a massage, herb-infused steam, body scrub, or nail treatment. G2O long

L'Espalier prides itself on using artisanal and New England ingredients.

held court on Newbury Street and built up a good reputation there. It moved to a state-of-the-art space in 2018 with more options for pampering. ⏱ *2–3 hr. 33 Exeter St.* ☎ *617/262-2220. www.g2ospasalon. com. Mon–Tues 8am–8pm, Wed–Fri 8am–9pm, Sat 8am–6pm, Sun 10am–6pm. T: Copley.*

❼ Amble through the Boston Public Garden. We reference the Public Garden a lot in this book, but that's because it's the jewel of the city. In addition to being a destination for historians and for kids, it's also a wonderful spot for lovers (or wannabes). Especially at dusk, when the sky turns pink, its benches are the perfect location for a first kiss—or 10th or 10,000th. ⏱ *30 min. See p 88.*

❽ Take in a concert at Jordan Hall. While its neighbor Symphony Hall (p 132) has more grandeur, Jordan Hall, on the campus of New England Conservatory, is also a beautiful venue with wonderful acoustics. The schedule is primarily classical, but the hall also books special events like Cuban jazz and lots of student recitals. Most of the programs are not just top quality, but free. ⏱ *2 hr. See p 125.*

❾ Stroll along and around Charles Street. Beacon Hill is one of the most enjoyable areas in the city for wandering, and its small-scale commercial street is good for window shopping and daydreaming. Stroll 2 short blocks up either of the side streets Mt. Vernon or Pinckney to **Louisburg Square,** one of the poshest residences in the city. The celebrated 19th-century singer Jenny Lind—promoted as the "Swedish Nightingale" by impresario P. T. Barnum—married her accompanist in the parlor of 20 Louisburg Square in 1852. ⏱ *30 min. See p 16,* ❷.

❿ Check into the Eliot. Boston has more than its share of elegant lodgings to choose from, but the Eliot Hotel, at the corner of Commonwealth and Massachusetts avenues, is a perennial favorite. It is independently owned and evocative of Brahmin splendor without breaking the bank. Rooms are outfitted with cozy beds, Italian marble bathrooms, and bathrobes for two. Its busy Japanese restaurant, UNI, is overseen by celebrity chef Ken Oringer and open for breakfast and dinner—with late-night ramen available Friday and Saturday. *See p 139.*

The narrow streets of Beacon Hill are perfect for a romantic stroll.

⑪ Have a drink at Top of the Hub Jazz Lounge. On the 52nd floor of Boston's soaring Prudential Tower, Top of the Hub's dining room and lounge both offer spectacular views in a swank setting. Evenings after 7:30, the lounge features jazz ensembles—just the atmosphere for a fancy cocktail, if that's your style. ⏱ *2–3 hr. See p 118.*

⑫ Dance under the stars at the ICA. You'll have to check the Institute of Contemporary Art calendar to confirm options, but in the past the museum has hosted nighttime swing dancing, Caribbean dance parties, and an annual "White Hot" event in August where most guests dress top to bottom in white. Parties are usually held Friday nights from 5 to 10pm and take place on the large harborside patio. ⏱ *2–3 hr. See p 25,* ⑦. ●

Beacon Hill & Back Bay

1 Massachusetts State House
2 Museum of African American History
3 Otis House
4 Nichols House Museum
5 Louisburg Square
6 Acorn Street
7 Charles Street
8 Beacon Hill Hotel and Bistro
9 First Church in Boston
10 First Baptist Church
11 Hotel Vendome Fire Memorial
12 Burrage House
13 Skywalk Observatory
   at the Prudential Center

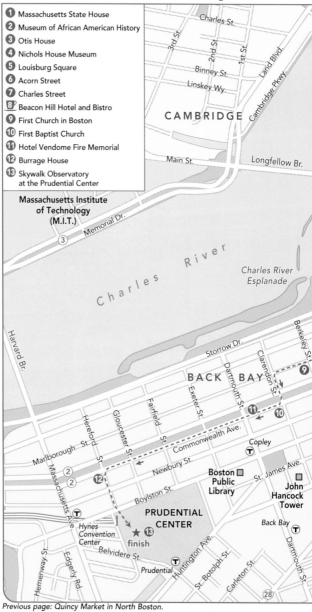

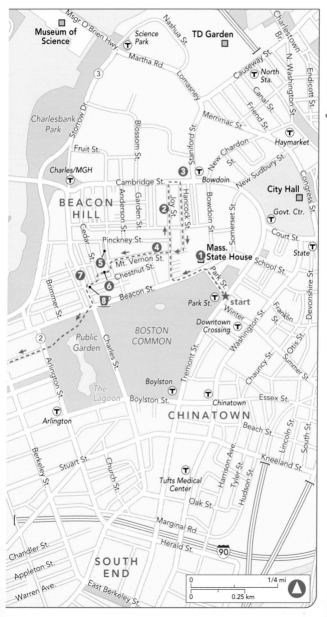

With its Federalist townhouses and mansions, and narrow, cobblestone streets, Beacon Hill is pretty as a picture. It also has a rich history as an important enclave for the Abolition Movement and a stop on the Underground Railroad, the network of secret safe houses used by African-American slaves to escape into freedom. West of Beacon Hill, Back Bay spreads out in a grid of streets, in contrast with the crazy-quilt geography of the city's older neighborhoods. This area was created by landfill projects executed between 1835 and 1882, replacing a marshy body of water. Streets here go in alphabetical order, starting at the Public Garden with Arlington Street on to Berkeley Street, Clarendon Street, and so on. You may not be able to gain entrance to the churches on this route, but the exteriors are worth a look. START: **Park Street.**

❶ ★ **Massachusetts State House.** The construction of the golden-domed state capitol, which opened in 1798, coincided with the emergence of Beacon Hill as a fashionable neighborhood. The building is prototypical Boston: red brick with white marble trim. Its iconic status can be credited to Charles Bulfinch, the best-known architect of the Federal era (1780–1820). He also designed several graceful residences highlighted on this tour. *See p 35,* ❸.

❷ ★★ kids **Museum of African American History.** "Boston's Second Revolution"—the fight against slavery and for the equality of African-Americans—was led in the 1800s by free blacks who made

their home on Beacon Hill and Boston's West Side. They were leaders in the Abolition Movement, the Underground Railroad, the U.S. Civil War, and the earliest efforts to bring education and full rights to black Americans. This fascinating museum highlights this history. It occupies the **Abiel Smith School** (1834), the first American public grammar school for African-American children, and the **African Meeting House** (1806), one of the oldest black churches in the country. Changing and permanent exhibits use art, artifacts, documents, historic photographs, and other objects to explore an important era that often takes a back seat in Revolutionary War–obsessed

The Massachusetts State House features a dome that's gilded in gold leaf.

Beacon Hill's Black History

Beacon Hill is best known for its gaslights, cobblestones and black-iron fences. It's less known for its ethnically diverse past. The north side of "The Hill" was home to free blacks from the West Indies and Africa in the 1600s, before Brahmin Boston moved in. In the 1800s and 1900s, men and women in Boston's free African-American community were leaders in the national fight to end slavery and to achieve equality. During the Civil War, black Bostonians formed the core of the 54th Massachusetts Regiment, fighting alongside white soldiers to preserve the country's union and take down slavery. The **Robert Gould Shaw and 54th Massachusetts Regiment Memorial** (p 35, ❷) in the Boston Common commemorates their service. **Boston's Black Heritage Trail** (www.maah.org/trail.htm and www.nps.gov/boaf) is a 1.6-mile walking tour of important sites on Beacon Hill and was developed by the **Museum of African American History** ❷ in partnership with the city of Boston and National Park Service. Ranger-led tours are available in summer, and self-guided tours are available on the websites.

New England. Be sure to visit Holmes Alley, off Smith Court—the narrow passageway is believed to have been a hiding place for fugitive slaves traveling the Underground Railroad. Guided tours of **Boston's Black Heritage Trail** tour conclude here. ⏱ 1 hr. 46 Joy St. ☎ 617/725-0022. www.maah.org. Admission $10 adults, $8 seniors & students, free for kids 12 & under. Mon–Sat 10am–4pm. Tours of Boston's Black Heritage Trail led by National Park Service rangers begin in Boston Common & end here: Information is at ☎ 617/742-5415 and www.nps.gov/boaf. T: Park St.

❸ ★★ **Otis House.** This magnificent 1796 Federal-style mansion was the first of three designed for Harrison Gray Otis by his friend Charles Bulfinch, who two years later completed the **Massachusetts State House** ❶. An engrossing tour touches on the history of the neighborhood, discusses historic preservation, and shows off the house and its

furnishings. The architectural details share the spotlight with the story of a young family bound for bigger things: Harrison Otis was a real estate developer who was later a congressman and mayor of Boston, and Sally Foster Otis appointed their home in grand style and enjoyed a reputation for entertaining lavishly. This house is actually just across the street from where Beacon Hill ends, in Bowdoin Square in Boston's West End neighborhood. ⏱ 1 hr. 141 Cambridge St.; enter from Lynde St. ☎ 617/994-5920. www.historicnewengland.org/property/otis-house. Tours $10 adults, $9 seniors, $5 students, free for Boston residents. Apr–Nov Wed–Sun 11am–4:30pm, with tours on the half hour. Closed Dec–Mar. T: Charles/MGH.

❹ ★ **Nichols House Museum.** Beacon Hill proper retains a fair number of one-family homes. Almost all of the private residences on the narrow streets of "the Hill" are tantalizingly close yet inaccessible to visitors.

This 1804 building, which is attributed to architect Charles Bulfinch (again), is the only one that can be visited (by guided tour only). The tour permits a glimpse of Boston during the lifetime of the house's most famous occupant, Rose Standish Nichols (1872–1960), a suffragist, feminist, pacifist, and pioneering landscape designer. Nichols traveled the world, returning home with many of the art works and artifacts that decorate her house, which became a museum after her death. ⏱ *45 min. 55 Mount Vernon St.* ☎ *617/227-6993. www.nichols housemuseum.org. Tours $10 adults, $8 seniors, $5 students, free for kids 12 & under. Apr–Oct Tues–Sat 11am–4pm, Nov–Mar Thurs–Sat 11am–4pm; tours start every hour on the hour. T: Park St.*

⑤ ★ **Louisburg Square.** The fanciest addresses in Boston's fanciest neighborhood surround the namesake park—pronounced "lewisburg"—which sits within a daunting iron fence. Louisa May Alcott lived at #10 after the successful publication of her *Little Women.* Circle the square to take in the beauty of the location. See p 16, ❸. ⏱ *10 min.*

Homes on Beacon Hill's exclusive Louisburg Square.

Between Mount Vernon St. (at Willow St.) & Pinckney St. (at Grove St.).

⑥ ★★ **kids Acorn Street.** Compact, unspoiled, and adorable, this cobblestone lane feels like a surprise. The relatively smaller homes here face the garden walls of larger properties behind them and once housed tradesmen who serviced the neighborhood's wealthier clients. Needless to say, that's no longer the case: The townhouse at #3 Acorn sold in 2016 for $3.7 million. *Between Willow & W. Cedar sts.*

⑦ ★★ **kids Charles Street.** In other cities, a street with this central location and tourist flow might have capitulated to T-shirt shops and knick-knack stores. Instead, merchants here continue to serve their neighbors as well as visitors, with an appealing collection of bakeries, antique shops, restaurants, and taverns. ⏱ *15 min.*

⑧ ★★ **Beacon Hill Hotel and Bistro.** This graceful restaurant always produces memorable meals, from sandwiches and salads to more elaborate dishes such as coq au vin and veal osso bucco. It's open daily for breakfast, lunch, dinner, and weekend brunch. *25 Charles St.* ☎ *800/640-3935. www.beaconhill hotel.com/boston-bistro. $$.*

⑨ ★ **First Church in Boston.** Located on Back Bay's Marlborough Street, a gracious residential thoroughfare, First Church in Boston is a direct successor of *the* first church in Boston. John Winthrop and his followers had barely landed when they adopted the covenant that launched the congregation in 1630. This building, designed to resemble an English country church, dates to 1867. A fire in 1968 destroyed much of the original building, but a 1971 renovation preserved much of the remaining structure. It's open for Sunday services and occasional concerts. ⏱ *5 min. 66 Marlborough St.* ☎ *617/267-6730. www.first churchboston.org. T: Arlington.*

⑩ ★ **First Baptist Church.** Inside a structure made with "Roxbury Puddingstone" granite and topped with a 176-foot tower, Louis Comfort Tiffany designed the stained-glass window depicting Jesus' baptism and three rose windows. ⏱ *5 min. 110 Commonwealth Ave.* ☎ *617/267-3148. www.first baptistchurchofboston.com. T: Arlington.*

⑪ ★ **Hotel Vendome Fire Memorial.** On June 17, 1972, fire devastated the former Hotel Vendome at 160 Commonwealth Avenue. The blaze had been extinguished and cleanup operations were under way when a section of the structure unexpectedly collapsed. Nine firefighters were killed—the worst tragedy in the department's history. The dramatic memorial is a low, curving black granite wall. Ted Clausen's design includes a bronze rendering of a firefighter's helmet and coat draped

Burrage House was inspired by Château de Chenonceau in France's Loire Valley.

First Baptist Church was designed by H. H. Richardson in the Romanesque Revival style.

over the wall. *Commonwealth Ave. at Dartmouth St.*

⑫ ★ **Burrage House.** As opulent as Boston can be, you don't see many turrets. Inspired by the Château de Chenonceau in France's Loire Valley, this 1899 mansion designed by Charles Brigham is a rare Boston example of over-the-top French Renaissance architecture— turrets and all. *314 Commonwealth Ave.*

⑬ ★ kids **Skywalk Observatory at the Prudential Center.** Having seen the Back Bay from street level, consider a new perspective from above. The 360° panorama from the 50th floor of the Prudential Tower affords views as far as New Hampshire and Cape Cod when the sky is clear. ⏱ *1 hr. 800 Boylston St.* ☎ *617/859-0648. www.skywalkboston.com. Daily 10am–8pm (until 10pm mid-Mar to early Nov); call to confirm opening, especially on cloudy days. Admission $19 adults, $15 seniors & students, $13 kids 3–12. See p 33 for CityPass discount ticket information. T: Prudential.*

The Seaport District

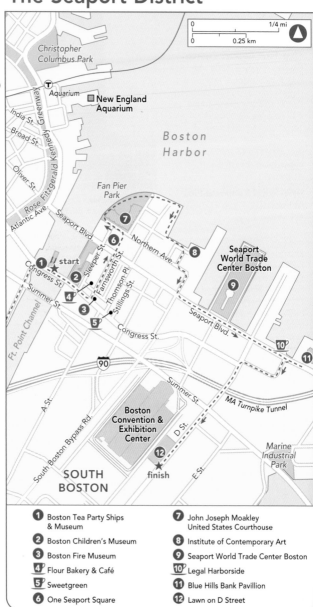

1. Boston Tea Party Ships & Museum
2. Boston Children's Museum
3. Boston Fire Museum
4. Flour Bakery & Café
5. Sweetgreen
6. One Seaport Square
7. John Joseph Moakley United States Courthouse
8. Institute of Contemporary Art
9. Seaport World Trade Center Boston
10. Legal Harborside
11. Blue Hills Bank Pavillion
12. Lawn on D Street

oston has had seaport activity in this part of the city for over 150 years, but a distinct "Seaport District" as a living/working/tourism destination only began to take shape at the turn of the 21st century. Encompassing a long stretch of South Boston waterfront and parallel roads, the area has blossomed into a hodgepodge of spanking-new luxury housing, retail spaces, and swank restaurants, bars, and hotels. A website by WS Development, www.boston seaport.xyz, helps keep track of what's new. The neighborhood blends into the Fort Point industrial district on the south side of the Fort Point Channel, where warehouses have been reclaimed as office space, artist studios, and loft condominiums. START: **South Station.**

1 ★ kids Boston Tea Party Ships & Museum. A lot of history about the American Revolution gets crammed into a visit here, culminating with visitors participating in a tea party re-enactment by tossing bales of fake tea overboard under the encouragement of costumed patriots. The panoramic movie that simulates battlefield action might be intense for young visitors. Tickets are pricey; check online for discounts. 🕐 1 hr. 306 Congress St. ☎ 866/955-0667. www. bostonteapartyship.com. Museum Apr–Oct daily from 10am (last tour 5pm); Nov–Mar last tour at 4pm. Gift shop & tea room open 1 hr. earlier & stay open 1 hr. later. Admission $28 adults, $25 seniors & students, $18 kids 5–12. T: South Station.

2 ★★★ kids Boston Children's Museum. A terrific play space for pre-school to early middle-school-age kids, with 3 floors or interactive exhibits for experimental and experiential fun. There's an area just for toddlers plus maker spaces, a bubble room, and lots of stuff to climb on and crawl through. 🕐 3–5 hr. See p 29, **1**.

3 ★ kids Boston Fire Museum. Small and open on a sporadic schedule, by all means step in if the doors are open. Housed in a former firehouse, the museum has artifacts from New England firehouses, metal toys, photographs, and amazing antique fire trucks. Be sure to see the very cool Ephraim Thayer Pumper, a vehicle constructed by Paul Revere in 1793. The volunteers are friendly and give out plastic fire hats to young visitors. 🕐 15 min. 344 Congress St. ☎ 617/338-9700. www.bostonfire museum.com. Free admission. T: Courthouse.

For a sweet treat, try **4 Flour Bakery + Cafe**—perhaps a sticky bun, cinnamon cream brioche, or lemon ginger scone? The cafe also has decadent sandwiches, salads, and grain bowls. 12 Farnsworth St. See p 104. If Flour is too crowded (the cafe is small), head to **5 Sweetgreen** for a fancy salad to go. 372 Congress St. See p 109.

6 ★ One Seaport Square. A gigantic mixed-use project still in the making, this complex includes 832 luxury rental units in two towers (The Benjamin, at 25 Northern Ave., and VIA, at 5 Fan Pier Blvd.) and three stories of retail and dining. **The Grand** nightclub (p 118) and **ShowPlace Icon** movie theater (p 127) are both here, too. Northern Ave. & Seaport Blvd., at Fan Pier Blvd. ☎ 617/338-9700. www. bostonseaport.xyz. T: Courthouse.

7 ★ kids John Joseph Moakley United States Courthouse. After visiting the Fort Point neighborhood earlier in this tour, it's time to head to the sea. Make your way to the harbor side of this spectacular federal courthouse for the best views of the stunning building. An 88-foot-tall curved glass wall cradles a 2.25-acre public space, **Fan Pier Park,** and the adjacent **Harborwalk** path, which is especially attractive in this stretch. New in 1999, the courthouse helped usher in the redevelopment of the Seaport District. There are public galleries and exhibits throughout the building for visitors to explore. ⏱ *20 min. 1 Courthouse Way.* ☎ *617/261-2440. www.moakley courthouse.com. Free admission. T: Courthouse.*

8 ★★ kids Institute of Contemporary Art. Also on the Harborwalk and, like the Moakley Courthouse **7**, a stunning building from harbor side, the ICA was a pioneer when it moved here from its former Back Bay home in 2006. Then, it was the lone "tall" building in a sea of parking lots. Now, like the protagonist in Virginia Lee Burton's 1942 children's book, *The Little House,* it is a pipsqueak among skyscrapers. Still, the art inside is innovative. ⏱ *2 hr. See p 25,* **7***.*

9 ★ World Trade Center Boston. Yes, Boston has a World Trade Center. It's a base for the U.S. Export Assistance Center and offices of the U.S. Department of Commerce. Exhibitions and conventions take place here, both for the international trade industry and for just about any organization under the sun, from the Run to Remember to the Extreme Beer Fest. **Spirit of Boston** (☎ 617/748-1450; www.spiritcruises.com/boston) and **Bay State Cruise Company** (☎ 617/748-1428; www.baystatecruisecompany.com) are both docked here, too, at 200 Seaport Blvd.—see p 13. ⏱ *10 min. 164 Northern Ave. www.wtca.org/world-trade-center-boston & www.seaportboston.com. Free admission. T: World Trade Center.*

There are three stories of waterside dining at the massive **10 Legal Harborside**: A casual restaurant with a large outside patio on the

The ICA was founded in 1936 as a sister institution to New York's MoMA and moved to its new location in 2006.

Blue Hills Bank Pavilion.

first floor, a formal restaurant on the second floor, and a rooftop bar with a sushi menu. *270 Northern Ave., on Liberty Wharf. See p 117.*

⓫ ★★ Blue Hills Bank Pavilion. In the summertime, this outdoor amphitheater next door to the giant **Liberty Wharf** (www.liberty wharf.co) restaurant space—which includes not just **Legal Harborside** (p 117) but Del Frisco's Double Eagle Steak House, Temazcal Tequila Cantina, Tony C's Sports Bar & Grill, and 75 bistro, as well—is a fun spot to catch a concert. *290 Northern Blvd. See p 119.*

⓬ ★★ kids Lawn on D Street. South of the waterfront is South Boston, a dense residential area showcased in the 1997 movie *Good Will Hunting* (which still holds up— "My boy's wicked smaht"). Midway between the Seaport and Southie is the charming Lawn on D Street. It's an urban playground with a grassy lawn, food concessions, and occasional live music and festivals. Young adults throng to here at night to chillax on huge glow-in-the-dark swings. *420 D St.* ☎ *877/393-3393. www.signature boston.com/lawn-on-d. Free admission. T: World Trade Center & 10-min. walk.*

Jamaica Plain & the Zoo

1 The Emerald Necklace and Jamaica Pond
2 Samuel Adams Boston Brewery
3 Centre Street
4 Tres Gatos
5 Arnold Arboretum
6 Forest Hills Cemetery
7 Franklin Park Zoo
8 Doyle's Café

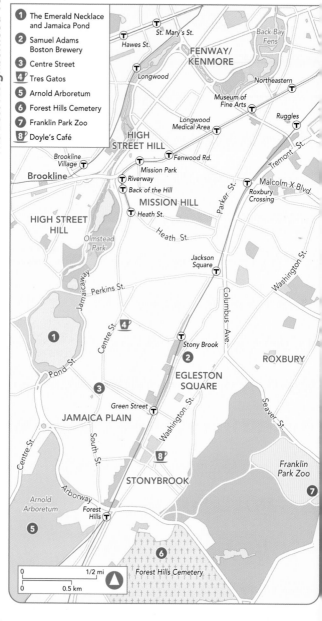

With its scenic Jamaica Pond and world-class Arnold Arboretum, Jamaica Plain reigns as one of Boston's most livable—and diverse—neighborhoods. Many of the 140 languages spoken in Boston can be heard in this borough, where more than 20 percent of residents speak Spanish. In the Victorian era city dwellers summered here, and their ornate homes still stand in a bright flourish of colors. In recent decades, J.P. (as it's known to locals) has become an enclave for hipsters and LGBTQ families. Located beyond the typical tourist haunts but easily accessible by the Orange Line, J.P. is a fine destination for any combination of the highlights below: Perhaps a stroll along quirky Centre Street and the nearby Jamaica Pond? A brewery tour and then a trolley ride to Doyle's pub? Outdoor time in the Harvard-run Arboretum or the nearby cemetery? Or maybe an afternoon at Boston's only zoo?

1 ★★ kids **The Emerald Necklace and Jamaica Pond.** The "Emerald Necklace" is a linked park system envisioned by landscape architect Frederick Law Olmsted some 120 years ago. Now an urban oasis, this green passageway functions just as he'd hoped. It's possible to bike or walk along a vehicle-free, tree-lined path from Boston Common in downtown to six other parks, traveling through the Fenway and past the Museum of Fine Arts, and ending in **Franklin Park** (p 69, **7**). You can stroll any or all of it yourself. (If you're game you can take a bike tour from the **Shattuck Visitor Center** operated by the Emerald Necklace Conservancy, located close to the MFA's Fenway entrance.) Near the end of the 7-mile route is the sizable and surprisingly peaceful **Jamaica Pond.** This spring-fed kettle pond once supplied city drinking water and its frozen blocks were harvested for ice. A separate 1.5-mile loop encircles Jamaica Pond and a boathouse offers sailboat and rowboat rentals from April through mid-November. *Emerald Necklace's Shattuck Visitor Center; 125 The Fenway.* ☎ *617/522-2700. www.emeraldnecklace.org. Mon–Fri 9am–5pm year-round, plus*

Spring-fed Jamaica Pond once supplied drinking water to Bostonians.

Sat–Sun 11am–4pm May–Oct. T: Northeastern. Jamaica Pond: 507 Jamaica Way (Pond St.). www.boston. gov/parks/jamaica-pond. T: Green St.

2 ★★ **Samuel Adams Boston Brewery.** Tucked into an area known as the Brewery Complex and situated in the old Haffenreffer Brewery, this is the smallest of Samuel Adams' three beer-making locations and the only one that hosts tours. The company's suds started flowing in 1984, not in the revolutionary era as some suppose. But founder Jim Koch tapped into the patriotic fervor that Boston historically had for beer. Before prohibition this stretch of Jamaica Plain and neighboring Roxbury boasted the most breweries per capita in the U.S. The free tours are fun and last about an hour (arrive early—tickets are offered on a first-come, first-served basis) and the visit can be extended to the taproom or beer garden. There's a gift shop on site. *30 Germania St. www.samuel adams.com. Tours Mon–Thurs & Sat 10am–3pm, Fri 10am–5:30pm. T: Stony Brook.*

3 ★ **kids Centre Street.** The eclectic businesses along J.P.'s main artery reflect the neighborhood's slow-cooked gentrification, where old-school barbershops abut organic eateries and thrift shops neighbor frilly pet boutiques. Along Centre between Pond and Eliot streets, you'll find the flagship ice cream shop for **JP Licks** (659 Centre)—order anything with their unforgettable hot fudge. Don't mind the chaotic window displays at **George's Shoes** (669 Centre)—its cramped quarters always boast great markdowns. Find a well-proportioned sandwich at **City Feed and Supply** (672 Centre) or a gently worn book or sweater at **Boomerangs** (716 Centre). Keep walking past Eliot as Centre turns into

South, and you'll find a quirky record store **Deep Thoughts JP** (138-B South St.). *Centre St. between Pond & Eliot sts. & South St. between Boynton & Hall sts. www.jpcentresouth.com. T: Green St.*

Local favorite **4** **Tres Gatos**, about a 15-minute walk north of the intersection of Centre and Eliot streets, has smoky cocktails and tapas dining and oh—there's also a book and record shop! Check the calendar for occasional live music. It's open for dinner and weekend brunch. Its recommended Italian-inspired sister restaurant, Centre Street Café (669a Centre St.), serves lunch on Fridays, brunch on the weekend, and dinner nightly. *470 Centre St.* ☎ *617/477-4851. www. tresgatosjp.com. $–$$.*

5 ★★★ **kids Arnold Arboretum.** A spectacular jewel along the Emerald Necklace, the Arnold Arboretum of Harvard University is a living museum of North American and Asian plant species and a natural retreat for locals and visitors. Paved and dirt trails weave in and out of towering conifers, hardy rhododendrons, and centenarian trees (100 years and older). There's reason to explore year-round, whether to smell the fragrant lilacs on **Lilac Sunday** (celebrated annually in early May since 1908) or gawk at the impeccable bonsai collection (on view Apr–Oct). After a snowfall the woodsy hills quickly fill with snowshoe and cross-country ski tracks. Because it's operated by Harvard University, there are ample opportunities to learn, including self-guided tours for kids or adults. Private tours can be arranged about 3 weeks in advance. The **Hunnewell Building Visitor Center** has a giant relief map and is

Harvard's Arnold Arboretum is the second largest "link" in Olmsted's Emerald Necklace, occupying 281 acres.

wheelchair accessible, including the restrooms on the ground floor. *125 Arborway.* ☎ *617/524-1718. www. arboretum.harvard.edu. Open daily sunrise to sunset. Free admission. Hunnewell Building: Mon–Fri 9am–5pm, Sat–Sun 10am–5pm, closed holidays. T: Forest Hills.*

⑥ ★ Forest Hills Cemetery.

Forest Hills was designed to be a place of beauty for the living. Among its rolling hills and mature trees are architectural and sculptural gems that symbolize its 19th-century intentions. A resting place for prominent citizens like poets e.e. cummings and Anne Sexton, as well as abolitionist William Lloyd Garrison, it's still an active burial ground. *95 Forest Hills Ave.* ☎ *617/524-0128. www.foresthills cemetery.com. Gates open 7am year-round, closing hours change seasonally. T: Forest Hills.*

⑦ ★ kids Franklin Park Zoo.

This small zoo is located in Franklin Park, Boston's largest city park. The warthog and wildebeest live in the area called Serengeti Crossing and the lion and tiger live in Kalahari Kingdom. There's a large, appealing playground here, too. The biggest stink is made about the giant Corpse flowers, which may or may not bloom in a given year. The stench they give off is unbearable but the experience is unforgettable. We recommend driving (there's free parking) or taking a cab. The entrance is on the far eastern side of the park. *1 Franklin Park Rd.* ☎ *617/541-5466. www.zoonew england.org. Mon–Fri 10am–5pm, Sat–Sun 10am–6pm Apr–Sept; daily 10am–4pm Oct–Mar. T: Forest Hills.*

⑧ Doyle's Cafe.

The pub of pubs in a city full of 'em. Politicians have been coming here since 1882—lots of varnished wood and brass give the room its weathered patina—and the first Sam Adams was served here. A trolley shuttle brings tourists from the Samuel Adams Brewery (②, p 68). There are plenty of tables for groups and the kitchen turns out standard pub grub. *3484 Washington St.* ☎ *617/524-2345. www.doylescafeboston. com. Mon–Tues 11am–midnight, Wed–Thurs 11am–12:30am, Fri–Sat 9am–12:30am, Sun 9am–midnight. $–$$.*

Harvard Square

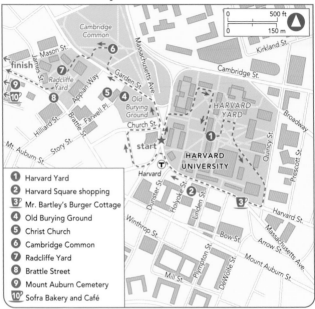

1 Harvard Yard
2 Harvard Square shopping
3' Mr. Bartley's Burger Cottage
4 Old Burying Ground
5 Christ Church
6 Cambridge Common
7 Radcliffe Yard
8 Brattle Street
9 Mount Auburn Cemetery
10' Sofra Bakery and Café

To be clear, Harvard Square isn't a square or even a plaza—it's only the intersection of Massachusetts Avenue, Brattle Street, and John F. Kennedy Street, with a subway stop and small concrete island at its center. No matter. The tightly packed surrounding streets make up a shopping and dining hub. Harvard University's undergraduate campus dominates "the Square" proper, with classrooms, dorms, and some of the oldest buildings in the country located just on the other side of a black wrought-iron fence. In the coldest winter months, the streets are busy, and once spring comes, they explode with activity—outdoor cafes, street musicians, and bug-eyed students who are grateful to take a break from staring at computer screens. START: **Harvard T.**

1 ★★ kids **Harvard Yard.** The oldest college in the country, founded in 1636, Harvard welcomes visitors and offers free guided tours. Even without a guide, the stately main campus—two adjoining quads known as Harvard Yard—is interesting to walk through. The most popular stop is the **John Harvard statue** in front of **University Hall.** The quad they're in is mostly undergraduate dorms, but stroll to the northwestern corner to see **Holden Chapel.** It's a

tiny Georgian building, completed in 1744, which served temporarily the barracks for Revolutionary War troops serving under George Washington, and later an anatomy lab. Today it's a rehearsal space for undergraduate choral groups.

Walk around University Hall into the second quad and work your way clockwise. **Memorial Church** (🕐 617/495-5508) was dedicated in 1932. Nondenominational Protestant services (including morning prayer Mon–Sat 8:45–9am during the academic year and Sun services at 11am) are open to the public. **Sever Hall** (rhymes with "fever") was designed by H. H. Richardson, the mastermind of Boston's Trinity Church. Architects rave about the brickwork, the chimneys, the roof, and even the window openings. If you stand next to one side of the front door and whisper into the archway, the person next to you won't hear a thing but someone at the other end of the arch can hear you loud and clear. The majestic **Widener Library** has a dramatic front stairway. It holds, it says, one of the world's most comprehensive research collections in the humanities and social sciences, in more

John Harvard statue in Harvard Yard.

than 100 languages. It's not open to the public.

At the time of writing, the **Smith Campus Center,** just outside of the Yard behind the library and the surrounding iron fence, was schedule to open in fall 2018. The center will house a visitor center as well as a plaza with cafe seating along Massachusetts Avenue, at Dunster Street. 🕐 *30 min. Smith Campus Center, 1350 Massachusetts Ave.* ☎ *617/495-1000. www.harvard.edu/ on-campus/visit-harvard/tours. Tours Mon–Sat; check website for schedule. T: Red Line to Harvard.*

2 🔲 **kids Harvard Square shopping.** The Square is like a circular bicycle wheel, with streets, like spokes, emanating from every direction. A cluster of particularly agreeable shops is in or within a few blocks of the epicenter (see chapter 4 for our favorites). 🕐 *1 hr. A full list of shops is online at www. harvardsquare.com/shops, the website of the Harvard Square Business Association.*

3 ★★★ **kids Mr. Bartley's Burger Cottage.** Elaborate burgers are the thing here, along with onion rings, sweet potato fries, and frappes—the regional name for milkshakes. If it's a Sunday or Monday, when Bartley's is closed, or if you're looking for healthier fare, head to Clover down the block (p 103). *1246 Massachusetts Ave.* ☎ *617/354-6559. www.mrbartley. com. $–$$.*

4 ★ **Old Burying Ground.** Sometimes called the Cambridge Burying Ground, this cemetery has been here since 1635, a year before the founding of the university. The evolving fashions in gravestones are on display here, with some 2 centuries' worth of examples. 🕐 *20* min. Corner of Massachusetts Ave. & Garden St. www.cambridgema.gov/theworks/ourservices/cambridgecemetery/oldburialground.

5 ★ **Christ Church.** The oldest standing church building in Cambridge was designed by Peter Harrison and opened in 1761. It's wooden, with a distinctive square tower. It originally had 44 high-backed box pews, which were purchased by individual parishioners. They were replaced in the 1850s with the pews that are there today, using much of the original wood. Today the church has an active Episcopal congregation. ⏱ *10 min. Zero Garden St.* ☎ *617/876-0200. www.cccambridge.org.*

6 ★ kids **Cambridge Common.** In 1631, a year after the founding of Newtowne (later named Cambridge), this public park was established. Today the Common covers 16 acres and includes the large **Alexander W. Kemp Playground,** a playing field, bike paths, and plenty of open space for lounging. The tall memorial commemorates the American Civil War, with a statue of Abraham Lincoln in an interior covered space near the base and a statue of a soldier on top. *Massachusetts Ave. & Garden St.*

7 ★ **Radcliffe Yard.** Founded as the Harvard Annex in 1879 and chartered as Radcliffe College in 1894, Harvard's "sister school" was a women's liberal arts college until 1999. Integration of women into Harvard classes began in the 1940s and accelerated in the 1970s, and in 1999 the institutions merged and the campus became home to the Radcliffe Institute for Advanced Study. The small Radcliffe Yard is an enclave of serenity, with redbrick buildings executed in typical New England college style (Greek Revival and Federal) surrounding a grass lawn. *10 Garden St. www.radcliffe.harvard.edu.*

8 ★★ **Brattle Street.** One of the most beautiful residential streets we've seen, Brattle Street has been an exclusive address since Colonial times. It gained fame—and the nickname "Tory Row"—around the time of the Revolution because of its association with British sympathizers. The loyalists later evacuated, but some of their lovely homes survive. The charming detour along Brattle Street (see map next page) will take you away from Harvard Square. Brattle Street curves to dead end at Mount Auburn at the final stop on this tour, a little more than a mile from Brattle and Mason. To return to Harvard Square you can pick up a 71 or 73 bus on Mount Auburn Street. ⏱ *45 min. Brattle St. from Mason St. to Mount Auburn St.*

The former Brattle Street home of poet Henry Wadsworth Longfellow.

Brattle Street

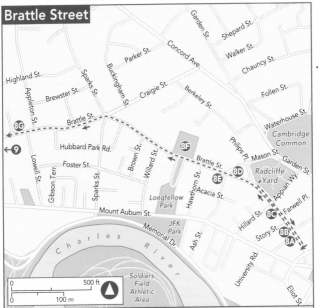

The 1727 **8A William Brattle House** (no. 42) is the property of the nonprofit Cambridge Center for Adult Education. A splash of modern design in Colonial Cambridge, the 1969 **8B Design Research Building** (no. 48) is the work of Benjamin Thompson and Associates. The Cambridge Center for Adult Ed also owns the **8C Hancock-Dexter-Pratt House** (no. 54), constructed in 1811 and immortalized by Longfellow, who saw the village blacksmith working here in the late 1830s, in his words, "under a spreading chestnut tree." The 1847 Gothic Revival **8D Burleigh House** is also known as the Norton-Johnson-Burleigh House (no. 85). Our old friend H. H. Richardson, architect of Boston's Trinity Church, designed the **8E Stoughton House** (no. 90), which was completed in 1883. A few steps further at No. 105 Brattle, the home of poet Henry Wadsworth Longfellow has been turned into the dual **8F Longfellow House–Washington's Headquarters National Historic Site** (☎ 617/876-4491; www.nps.gov/long). Longfellow lived here from 1843 until his death, in 1882. He was first here as a boarder in 1837, but after he married Fanny Appleton, her father made the house a wedding present. The home also served as George Washington's headquarters in 1775 and 1776, during the siege of Boston. The lovely grounds and gardens are open year-round to visitors, with free interior tours May to October. **8G Hooper-Lee-Nichols House** is at no. 159. The original section of this building was built around 1685, making it the second oldest house in Cambridge. It now contains the Cambridge Historical Society (☎ 617/547-4252; www.cambridgehistory.org).

❾ ★★ kids Mount Auburn Cemetery. Consecrated in 1831, Mount Auburn is a prime example of the "garden cemeteries" that gained popularity as urban centers became too congested to support the expansion of downtown burying grounds. It's a particularly beautiful combination of landscaping, statuary, sculpture, architecture, and history. Notable people buried here include museum founder Isabella Stewart Gardner, Christian Science founder Mary Baker Eddy, architect Charles Bulfinch, and abolitionist Charles Sumner. Mount Auburn is an active cemetery, so pets and picnicking are not allowed. There's a Visitors Center in Story Chapel at the front gate. Check the online event calendar for walks, talks, and special events. ⏱ *2 hr. 580 Mount Auburn St.* ☎ *617/547-7105. www.mount auburn.org. Daily summer 8am–8pm, winter 8am–5pm. Admission & self-guided tours free. T: Harvard; then bus no. 71 or 73.*

Mount Auburn's 175 acres hold some 5,000 trees representing 700-plus species.

If you've come this far out of Harvard Square, you might as well go one block further to the excellent **❿ ★★ Sofra Bakery and Cafe.** As this compact cafe notes in an equally compact way on its website, "sweet and savory tastes of Turkey, Lebanon and Greece are served here with a contemporary twist." It's the little sister to Oleana (p 107), on the other side of Cambridge. *1 Belmont St.* ☎ *617/661-3161. www. sofrabakery.com. $–$$.* ●

4 The Best Shopping

Shopping Best Bets

Out of Town News is an iconic newsstand in the center of Harvard Square.

Best **Museum Gift Shop**
★★ ICA Store, *25 Harbor Shore Drive (p 84)*

Best **Farmers' Market**
★★ Boston Public Market, *100 Hanover St. (p 85)*

Best **Contemporary Art Gallery**
★★ Krakow Witkin Gallery, *10 Newbury St. (p 77)*

Best **Bookstore with In-house Cafe**
★★ Trident Booksellers and Café, *338 Newbury St. (p 80)*

Best **Quirky T-Shirts**
★★ Johnny Cupcakes, *279 Newbury St. (p 83)*

Best **Sweet Treats**
★★ Beacon Hill Chocolates, *91 Charles St. (p 84)*

Best **Source for Red Sox Merch**
★★ Red Sox Team Store, *19 Yawkey Way. (p 83)*

Best **Unique Souvenir: Gurgling Cod Pitcher**
★★ Shreve, Crump & Low, *39 Newbury St. (p 85)*

Previous page: Beautiful Newbury Street has something for everyone.

Best **Shopping Destination for Families**
★★★ Faneuil Hall Marketplace, *4 S. Market St. (p 86)*

Best **Shopping for Tweens**
★ Newbury Comics, *332 Newbury St. (p 86)*

Best **Children's Clothing**
★ The Red Wagon, *69 Charles St. (p 81)*

Best **Thrift Store**
★ Boomerangs, *1407 Washington St. (p 81)*

Best **Retro Home Accessories**
★★ Black Ink, *101 Charles St. (p 84)*

Best **Toy Store**
★ Magic Beans, *Shops at Prudential Center, 776 Boylston St. (p 81)*

Best **Gallery and Art Destination**
★★★ SoWa Art + Design District, *460 Harrison Ave. (p 80)*

Harvard Square Shopping

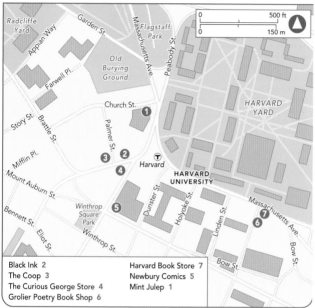

Black Ink **2**
The Coop **3**
The Curious George Store **4**
Grolier Poetry Book Shop **6**

Harvard Book Store **7**
Newbury Comics **5**
Mint Julep **1**

Shopping A to Z

Art Galleries

★ **Galería Cubana** SOUTH END Cuban art direct from the island, in a huge variety of vibrant styles and media, makes this a can't-miss destination. Weekends only (Sat–Sun 11am–6pm). *460 Harrison Ave.* ☎ *617/292-2822. www. lagaleriacubana.com. T: Back Bay, 15-min. walk.*

★ **International Poster Gallery** SOUTH END Glorious art nouveau posters, vintage travel posters from 1890 to 1940, popular Art Deco French classics, plus film, food, and sports images are on display here. After 23 years on Newbury Street, the Gallery moved in 2017 to SoWa, Boston's art and design neighborhood in the city's South End (see SoWa Art + Design District, below). *460C Harrison Ave. Suite C20.* ☎ *617/375-0076. www. internationalposter.com. T: Back Bay, 15-min. walk.*

★★ **Krakow Witkin Gallery** BACK BAY This venerable gallery is a destination for minimal contemporary art—paintings, prints, multimedia art, and sculpture. It hosts several exhibitions at a time and represents internationally known artists such as Bernd and Hilla Becher, Jenny Holzer, and Sol LeWitt and important local artists such as Suara Welitoff. *10 Newbury St.* ☎ *617/262-4490. www.krakow witkingallery.com. T: Arlington.*

Boston Shopping

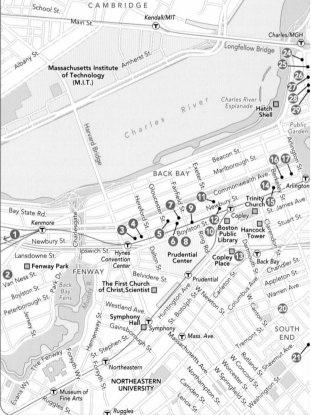

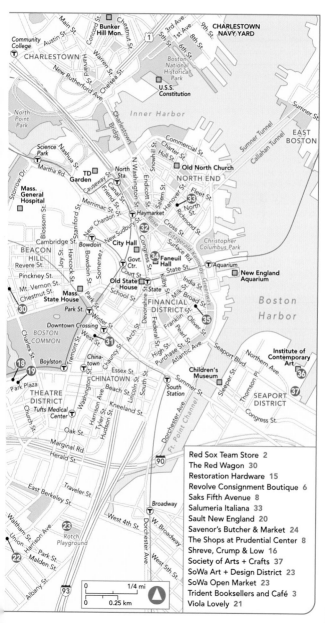

Red Sox Team Store 2
The Red Wagon 30
Restoration Hardware 15
Revolve Consignment Boutique 6
Saks Fifth Avenue 8
Salumeria Italiana 33
Sault New England 20
Savenor's Butcher & Market 24
The Shops at Prudential Center 8
Shreve, Crump & Low 16
Society of Arts + Crafts 37
SoWa Art + Design District 23
SoWa Open Market 23
Trident Booksellers and Café 3
Viola Lovely 21

★★ Society of Arts + Crafts

SEAPORT DISTRICT With a move in 2016 to 9,000 sq. ft. of retail, exhibition, and program space in the hot Seaport District, the Society has new opportunity to expose even more people to contemporary craft. It was founded in 1897 and its mission today is "to encourage the creation, collection, and promotion of the work of contemporary craft artists and to advance public appreciation of fine craft." It's located just next to the Institute of Contemporary Art (p 25). *100 Pier 4, Suite 200.* ☎ *617/266-1810. www. societyofcrafts.org. T: Courthouse.*

★★★ SoWa Art + Design District

SOUTH END A cluster of warehouses has been converted to a community of contemporary art galleries, boutiques, design showrooms, and artist studios. The complex at 460 Harrison Ave. is home to 40-some spaces running along the perpendicular Thayer Street. Consider this the central starting point for the vibrant SoWa district (SoWa stands for "south of Washington" street). In this building are the **International Poster Gallery** (p 77) and **Galería Cubana** (p 77) as well as artisans who specialize in hand letterpress, beadwork, T-shirt design, and repurposed vintage clothing. *460 Harrison Ave. www. sowaboston.com/460-harrison-retail. T: Back Bay, 15-min. walk.*

Books

★ Brattle Book Shop

DOWNTOWN CROSSING This tidy little used-book dealer was established in 1825 and bills itself as "one of America's oldest and largest antiquarian book shops." Well organized and packed to the brims, it specializes in rare and collectible titles and uses the adjacent empty lot as an outdoor book stall in good weather. *9 West St.* ☎ *800/ 447-9595 or 617/542-0210. www. brattlebookshop.com. T: Downtown Crossing.*

★★ kids Brookline Booksmith

COOLIDGE CORNER Lots of events, tons of gifts, and an enthusiastic staff make this shop—located in neighboring Brookline—one of the area's best independent bookstores. *279 Harvard St., Brookline.* ☎ *617/566-6660. www.brookline booksmith.com. T: Coolidge Corner.*

★ The Coop

CAMBRIDGE Unlike the Harvard Book Store (above), the Coop is managed by the University. It has new books, a small cafe, and lots of Harvard merchandise. *1400 Massachusetts Ave.* ☎ *617/499-2000. www.thecoop. com. T: Harvard.*

★ Grolier Poetry Book Shop

CAMBRIDGE A Harvard Square mainstay founded in 1927, Grolier is an important player in the U.S. poetry world. *6 Plympton St.* ☎ *617/ 547-4648. www.grolierpoetry bookshop.org. T: Harvard.*

★★ kids Harvard Book Store

CAMBRIDGE Locally owned and independent from the University (despite both its name and URL), this bookstore is the gem of Harvard Square. It has new titles upstairs and a deep selection of remainders and used books downstairs. The shop hosts numerous author readings both in store and at larger venues nearby. An onsite machine prints books on demand. *1256 Massachusetts Ave.* ☎ *800/542-READ or 617/661-1515. www.harvard.com. T: Harvard.*

★★ Trident Booksellers and Café

BACK BAY A wonderful place to while away the hours. Trident is a favorite bookstore for many Bostonians, given its **in-house restaurant and bar** (with a 9-page menu), huge magazine selection,

Brattle Book Shop opened in 1825 and has an outdoor bookstall.

and clever event programming (example: a theme night based around the TV show *Parks and Recreation*). *338 Newbury St. ☎ 617/267-8688. www.tridentbookscafe.com. T: Hynes Convention Center.*

Children's Toys & Clothes

★ **kids The Curious George Store** CAMBRIDGE The children's books and toys here include a huge selection of items that feature the famous inquisitive monkey, whose creators, Margret and H.A. Rey, were longtime Cantabrigians. Margret was alive to see the original store open in 1996. The store's building, at the center of Harvard Square, is undergoing major renovation in 2018 and 2019, and the bookstore will be relocated within the building in summer 2019. *1 John F. Kennedy St. ☎ 617/547-4500. www.thecuriousgeorgestore.com. T: Harvard.*

★ **kids Magic Beans** BACK BAY The city location of this local chain carries a wide selection of creative, high-end toys by brands such as Green Toys and Bruder as well as plenty of baby gear. Its furniture includes Stokke and Oeuf brand cribs. *Shops at Prudential Center, 776 Boylston St. ☎ 617/383-8296. www.mbeans.com. T: Copley.*

★ **kids Mulberry Road** BACK BAY Chic and cozy, Mulberry Road focuses on clothes and gifts for children 8 and under. The boutique got new owners in 2016 who added events to their offerings such as wintertime braiding and caricature drawings during spring's Artweek Boston. *251 Newbury St. ☎ 617/859-5861. www.mulberryroad.com. T: Copley.*

★ **kids The Red Wagon** BEACON HILL This welcoming space overflows with toys and gorgeous, pricey clothing and shoes for infants to preteens. Perhaps a lobster sweater for $68? *69 Charles St. ☎ 617/523-9402. www.theredwagon.com. T: Charles/MGH.*

Fashion

★ **Anne Fontaine** BACK BAY The French designer's specialty is perfect blouses. A bit of black and grey sneaks in, but it's really all about elegant white blouses and tailored dress shirts. *280 Boylston St. ☎ 617/423-0366. www.annefontaine.com. T: Arlington.*

★ **Boomerangs** SOUTH END AIDS Action Committee of Massachusetts, founded in 1983, is an important health service organization in the city. It's funded in part by four non-profit thrift shops in

Boston Shopping Destinations

Looking to stroll and shop? Head to these shopping meccas:

Newbury Street: Boston's most celebrated retail street starts at the Boston Public Garden and runs west for 1 mile. At this end the real estate and merch are elegant and pricey (Tiffany, Chanel, Burberry). Shops get quirkier with each passing block (Johnny Cupcakes, Trident Booksellers & Café, Newbury Comics). The cross streets are alphabetical A through H (Arlington, Berkeley, Clarendon, etc.) before reaching Boston's main artery, Massachusetts Avenue.

Charles Street: This handsome street is the heart of romantic Beacon Hill, with its gaslights, cobblestones, and brick row houses. The ⅓-mile stretch from Cambridge Street to Beacon Street is chock-a-block with boutiques, antiques stores, and restaurants, plus practical outlets like a pharmacy and a hardware store.

Copley Place & Prudential Center Malls: These adjacent indoor malls are high-end and sprawling. Copley (at 100 Huntington Ave.) has Neiman Marcus, Barneys, and Stuart Weitzman. The Shops at Prudential Center (at 800 Boylston Street) include Saks Fifth Avenue, Vineyard Vines, and Microsoft Store. Also in "the Pru" is **Eataly,** a three-story emporium of Italian food and dining. There's another entrance at 800 Boylston St.

"Discount Block": Boylston Avenue between Berkeley and Clarendon streets has discount clothing stores Nordstrom Rack and Marshalls; H&M is just round the corner, on the same block of Newbury Street.

Faneuil Hall Marketplace: This tourist-centric indoor-outdoor complex features dozens of kiosks with tourist knickknacks and Boston memorabilia; chain stores including Yankee Candle Company and Uniqlo, and a standalone Sephora megastore—something for everyone. There's also a food court along with indoor and outdoor restaurant dining.

Boston and Cambridge, including this "Special Edition" outlet, which carries the most fashionable inventory. *1407 Washington St.* ☎ *617/456-0996. www.shopboomerangs.com. T: Union Park.*

★ **Castanet Designer Consignment** BACK BAY Up on the second floor of a Newbury Street brownstone, Castanet took over the space of long-running consignment shop The Closet (a popular option

for 38 years) in 2016. It carries on the same tradition of offering gently used high-end clothing. *175 Newbury St.* ☎ *617/536-1919. www.shopcastanet.com. T: Copley.*

★ **Crush Boutique** BEACON HILL Crush describes itself as a boutique for "the kind of girls who love NYC/LA silk collections, cocktail dresses + designer denim." This small shop features young designers at a good range of prices. *131*

Charles St. ☎ 617/720-0010. www.shopcrushboutique.com. T: Charles/MGH. Also at 264 Newbury St. ☎ 617/424-0010. T: Hynes Convention Center.

★ Helen's Leather Shop BEACON HILL
Leather bags, leather jackets, Western cowboy boots, Stetson hats, and photos of John Wayne make Helen's—in this location since 1969—a wonderfully oddball addition to Charles Street. 110 Charles St. ☎ 617/742-2077. www.helensleather.com. T: Charles/MGH.

★★ kids Johnny Cupcakes
BACK BAY   Clever marketing meets hip design: The trademark logo of this Boston-born designer is a cupcake-and-crossbones, and wares (T-shirts, socks, hats) are presented like display items in a space-age *pâtisserie.* Johnny Cupcakes terms itself the "world's first T-shirt bakery," and the founder is a hardcore metal musician turned savvy entrepreneur. T-shirts, many of which are limited edition, run about $36. 279 Newbury St. ☎ 617/375-0100. www.johnnycupcakes.com. T: Hynes Convention Center.

★ La Perla BACK BAY
Luxurious and wildly expensive lingerie from Italy, in gorgeous confections of silk and lace. 250 Boylston St. ☎ 617/423-5709. www.laperla.com. T: Arlington.

★★ Mint Julep CAMBRIDGE
The well-curated collection of candy-colored dresses, adorable separates, and sparkly jewelry at this boutique are youthful and Instagram-friendly—just like the clientele. 6 Church St. ☎ 617/576-6468. www.shopmintjulep.com. T: Harvard.

★ Peruvian Connection BACK BAY
The Boston branch of this small chain—just 6 stores in the U.S. and one in London—is a cozy nook for women's sweaters and

separates. Many items are made from alpaca—cashmerelike, and knit by artisans in Peru. 170 Newbury St. ☎ 857/753-4546. www.peruvianconnection.com. T: Copley.

★★ kids Red Sox Team Store
FENWAY   The official team store of the Boston Red Sox is open year-round and is gigantic—25,000 sq. ft. of Sox hats, shirts, and jerseys, Fenway Park merch, and game-used memorabilia. **Tours of Fenway Park,** at the stadium just across the street, begin and end here. 19 Yawkey Way. ☎ 800/336-9299. www.yawkeywaystore.com. T: Kenmore.

★ Revolve Consignment Boutique BACK BAY
As a general rule, consignment stores in swankier neighborhoods turn up better goods. That's the case here. This shop is one of six in the Revolve network, which rotates its goods among the stores. The result: continually fresh stock. 262 Newbury St. ☎ 617/262-0720 www.revolveboutiques.com. T: Copley.

★ Sault New England BACK BAY
Men's clothing, shaving

Johnny Cupcakes, the self-described world's first T-shirt bakery.

accessories, and other gifts for fashionable fellows make this small shop a go-to. The store and its offerings evoke upscale, seaside New England. *577 Tremont St.* ☎ *857/239-9434. www.saultne.com. T: Back Bay.*

★ **Viola Lovely** BACK BAY Stark, cool, and pricey, Viola Lovely is like Eileen Fisher's edgier and somewhat glummer little sister. *1409 Washington St.* ☎ *857/277-0746. www.violalovely.com. T: Back Bay.*

Food & Candy

★★ kids **Beacon Hill Chocolates** BEACON HILL High-end indulgence, whether you want a single sweet or a big box of deliciousness. Also available: locally made Italian gelato and *sorbetto* in such flavors as dulce de leche, salted caramel, and mango. *91 Charles St.* ☎ *617/725-1900. www.beaconhillchocolates.com. T: Charles/MGH.*

★ **Brix Wine Shop** FINANCIAL DISTRICT Reputable and recommended. In addition to this location a block off the Rose Kennedy Greenway near Rowes Wharf, there's a shop in the South End, at 1284 Washington St. *105 Broad St.* ☎ *617/542-2749. www.brixwineshop.com. T: Aquarium.*

★ **Fastachi Nuts** BEACON HILL This family-owned specialty store based in nearby Watertown hand-roasts gourmet nuts in small batches. It also sells nut butters (try the roasted pistachio) and hand-made chocolates. *83 Charles St.* (☎ *617/924-8787. www.fastachi.com. T: Charles/MGH.*

★★ **Salumeria Italiana** NORTH END The best Italian grocery store in town carries cheeses, meats, pastas, olives, olive oils, vinegars, fresh bread, and more. *151 Richmond St.* ☎ *617/523-8743. www.salumeriaitaliana.com. T: Haymarket.*

★ **Savenor's Butcher & Market** BEACON HILL A top-of-the-line butcher shop with a small gourmet market featuring a rich cheese selection, chocolates, and hearty sandwiches. Savenor's is a perfect picnic launching pad. *160 Charles St.* ☎ *617/723-6328. www.savenorsmarket.com. T: Charles/MGH.*

Home Accessories

★★ kids **Black Ink** BEACON HILL A constantly changing stock of funky gifts and household items, toys, jewelry, and office accessories means Black Ink is never the same twice. This delightful independent business has a second shop in Harvard Square, at 5 Brattle St. *101 Charles St.* ☎ *617/497-1221. www.blackinkboston.com. T: Charles/MGH.*

★ **Crate & Barrel** BACK BAY Top-quality home accessories, kitchen items, and furniture in styles that range from funky to elegant. *777 Boylston St.* ☎ *617/262-8700. www.crateandbarrel.com. T: Copley.*

★★ **Restoration Hardware** BACK BAY Even if you're not in the market for a $489 duvet cover, this furniture and housewares store is worth a stop just to take in its architecture. The gloriously elegant 1863 neoclassical redbrick-and-brownstone building was originally a Museum of Natural History. See p 44. *234 Berkeley St.* ☎ *857/239-7202. www.rh.com. T: Arlington.*

Jewelry

★★ **ICA Store** SEAPORT DISTRICT The gift shop for the Institute of Contemporary Art (p 25) is expansive and fun, with elegant jewelry, quirky housewares, creative

A Gift That Says "Boston"

Need a good Boston souvenir? The unique **Gurgling Cod Pitcher** from Shreve, Crump & Low is fish-shaped, which causes its contents to give up a *glug-glug* when poured. Far prettier than it sounds, it's a touch of luxury from a business founded in 1796. **Red Sox caps** from the shops on Yawkey Way next to Fenway Park are good for baseball fans, and **"Harvard" T-shirts** from vendors on the Boston Common or Quincy Market are a smart option. Merchandise from the **USS Constitution** is a classy nautical choice, and **bean pots,** available at

Shreve, Crump & Low's Gurgling Cod pitchers have been around since 1964.

shop.osv.org, definitely say Boston. The Omni Parker House (p 142) invented the **Boston cream pie** in 1856 and will ship a modern version anywhere in the U.S. (it's actually not a pie but a cake filled with pastry cream and topped with chocolate). Feeling committed? Get a **"B" tattoo** in the font of the Boston Red Sox logo or a green three-leaf clover in the style of the Celtics. In a last-minute pinch, there's always a pink-and-orange **Dunkin' Donuts mug**—the franchise was founded in 1950, just 30 minutes away in Quincy—available at any of the bajillion locations in the city.

toys, and a huge collection of art and performance books. *25 Harbor Shore Drive.* ☎ *617/478-3104. www.icastore.org. T: Courthouse.*

★★ Shreve, Crump & Low

BACK BAY   Boston's premier luxury goods store was founded in 1796, 41 years before Charles Lewis Tiffany and John B. Young started Tiffany & Co. in New York. It specializes in fine jewelry and watches. Its unique "Gurgling Cod" water pitchers are a hoot and modeled after a so-called English "glug jug." *39 Newbury St.* ☎ *617/267-9100.*

www.shrevecrumpandlow.com. T: Arlington.

Malls & Markets

★★ kids Boston Public Market

DOWNTOWN   With over 30 food venders year-round, this indoor farmers' market provides one-stop-shop access to local purveyors such as Boston Honey Company, Boston Smoked Fish Company, which sells stellar blue fish pate and smoked haddock, and Hopsters Alley for New England craft beer, cider, and spirits. *100 Hanover St.* ☎ *617/973-4909.*

Faneuil Hall Marketplace.

www.bostonpublicmarket.org. T: Haymarket.

★ **Copley Place** BACK BAY This sleek enclave of boutiques and luxury mall brands adjoins the Shops at Prudential Center (see below). See box p 82. *100 Huntington Ave.* ☎ *617/262-6600. www.shopcopleyplace.com. T: Back Bay.*

★★★ kids **Faneuil Hall Marketplace** DOWNTOWN Shoppers, some local but mostly from out of town, flock to this five-building indoor-outdoor marketplace. Check the pushcarts for items that are most unique to Boston. See box p 82. *North, Congress & State sts. & Atlantic Ave.* ☎ *617/523-1300. www.faneuilhallmarketplace.com. T: Government Center or Aquarium.*

★ kids **The Shops at Prudential Center** BACK BAY "The Pru" mixes high-end chain shops and boutiques with pushcarts holding novelty items in a sprawling, indoor mall. See box on p 82. *800 Boylston St.* ☎ *617/236-3100. www.prudentialcenter.com. T: Prudential.*

★★ kids **SoWa Open Market** SOUTH END From May through October, this lively outdoor marketplace combines an artisanal foods market, a crafts market, and a circle of food trucks. A beer garden, new in 2016, serves up local beers, ciders, and wines in a converted Trolley Barn at 540 Harrison Ave. There's often live music, and the whole shebang is fine for families and even pet friendly. Open Saturday and Sunday. *460 Harrison Ave. www.sowaopenmarket.com. T: Back Bay, 15-min. walk.*

Music & Novelties
★ kids **Newbury Comics** BACK BAY Yes, you can find comics, as well as LPs, and CDs—including imports and independent labels—at this regional powerhouse, but its 28 stores are also packed with pop culture novelty items, figurines, socks, and T-shirts. *332 Newbury St.* ☎ *617/236-4930. www.newburycomics.com. T: Hynes Convention Center. Additional locations at Faneuil Hall Marketplace & Harvard Square.* ●

Boston Public Garden & Boston Common

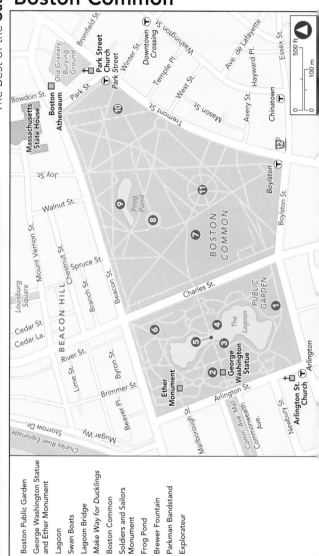

1 Boston Public Garden
2 George Washington Statue and Ether Monument
3 Lagoon
4 Swan Boats
5 Lagoon Bridge
6 Make Way for Ducklings
7 Boston Common
8 Soldiers and Sailors Monument
9 Frog Pond
10 Brewer Fountain
11 Parkman Bandstand
12 Explorateur

Previous page: Swan Boat rides in Boston Public Garden.

Together, the Boston Public Garden and the Boston Common are the heart of the city. The public parks are adjacent, but intersected by a busy thoroughfare. They have distinct personalities: Think of the Public Garden as Boston's front yard, carefully maintained and showy, and the Boston Common as the backyard, where the kids run around and play pickup baseball. Start at the primped Public Garden. START: **Arlington T.**

1 ★★★ kids Boston Public Garden. The 19th century left an indelible mark on Boston, and nowhere is that more permanent or more pleasant than in the Public Garden. The city set aside this land in the 1820s and the Garden was formally established in 1837. Working with a marshy riverbank and tons of landfill, the city created the nation's first public botanical garden. The gardens of Versailles inspired the original plan, and today, these 24 acres are crisscrossed with walkways and formally arranged flowers, trees, and shrubs, as well as five fountains. The exquisite flowerbeds change regularly, complementing the perennial plantings. Note that there are no restrooms in the Garden, but there are in the Common at 9 and 10. *www.friendsofthepublicgarden.org.*

2 ★★ kids George Washington Statue and Ether Monument. At the western side of the Garden, poised at the Commonwealth Avenue entrance, is the dramatic equestrian statue of George Washington. With a backdrop of the city skyline, it creates one of the most picturesque tableaus in Boston. It was unveiled in 1869 and has great personality. (See p 17, 6.) North of the Washington statue is the Ether Monument (1868), the oldest statue in the Public Garden. It celebrates the first use of general anesthesia in an operation, by Massachusetts General Hospital in 1846. The sculpture atop—an elaborate confection, in keeping with the fashion of the time—is John Quincy Adams Ward's depiction of the Good Samaritan. At the base, the streams of water that issue from the lions' heads represent healing.

3 ★★ kids Lagoon. Completed in 1861, the Garden's 3-acre lagoon

Exquisite flowerbeds in the Boston Public Garden change regularly, complementing perennial plantings.

The Public Garden's Lagoon is home to swans and ducks.

is a triumph of optical illusion—viewed from above, it's tiny, but from anywhere along the curving shore, it looks much more significant. Resembling an English pond, the lagoon today is home to the **Swan Boats** (see below), **live swans** (who spend the winter at **Franklin Park Zoo**, p 69, and whose annual return to the lagoon is celebrated with a brass-band-led parade), and numerous **ducks**.

④ ★★ kids Swan Boats. In keeping with the Victorian atmosphere of the rest of the Public Garden, these simple pedal-powered vessels (park employees do the work) each have an elaborate swan statue at the back, concealing the

pedaling mechanism and transforming a humble boat ride into an operatic fantasy. Robert Paget, who introduced the Swan Boats in 1877, was inspired by the swan-drawn boat in the Wagner opera *Lohengrin*. Leisurely rides around the lagoon take 12 to15 minutes. Outside of operating hours, the dock is still worth a look—at dusk, the berthed boats are one of the city's best photo ops. *Boston Public Garden.* ☎ *617/522-1966. www.swan boats.com. Tickets $4 adults, $2.50 kids 2–15, free for kids under 2. Open mid-Apr through early Sept. Daily 10am–4pm in spring and 10am–5pm in summer. T: Arlington.*

⑤ ★★ kids Lagoon Bridge. This diminutive footbridge, a popular site for wedding photos, sits at the heart of the Public Garden, surrounded by flowerbeds. Step away to the lagoon shore to appreciate the bridge's graceful proportions.

⑥ ★★ kids Make Way for Ducklings statues. Robert McCloskey's beloved 1941 book introduces young readers to Boston, where a family of ducks goes in search of a new place to live. After perilous adventures, they arrive at the Public Garden. Sculptor Nancy Schön's ducks were unveiled in 1987 on the 150th anniversary of the Garden. The bronze sculptures of the mother duck and her

The Boston Public Garden's bridge is one of the smallest suspension bridges in the world.

Children love the Make Way for Ducklings statues in the Boston Public Garden.

ducklings waddling in the direction of the water capture the imagination of just about everyone who encounters them—especially children, who are welcome to climb on them. Every Mother's Day in May, there's an adorable **Ducklings Parade** here for children in costume (p 159).

7 ★★ Boston Common. The Common has been in constant use since 1634, just a few years after the Puritans of the Massachusetts Bay Colony arrived from England. Over the years, these 45 acres have held pasture, barracks, parade grounds, ball fields, and more. The **Park Street subway stop** leads to the oldest subway line in the country, established in 1897 (it sometimes feels that ancient). In the wintertime, trees throughout the park are lit with twinkly colored lights. *www.friendsofthepublicgarden.org/ our-parks/the-common.*

8 ★★ Soldiers and Sailors Monument. The tall monument atop the highest point on the Common, Flagstaff Hill, commemorates Boston residents who died in the Civil War. The slope of the small hill is a popular spot for sunning.

9 ★★ kids Frog Pond. In Colonial times, real frogs lived in a body of water here. Today Frog Pond is a **spray pool** in the summer, beautiful **ice skating rink** in the winter, and **reflecting pool** in the spring and fall. *USA Today* readers in 2017

voted the ice rink the best in the U.S. and second best in North America (just behind Ottawa's Rideau Canal Skateway). A delightful **carousel** is on one side of the pond and a mid-sized **playground** on the other. There are **rest rooms** at the refreshment area. ☎ *617/635-2120 www.bostonfrogpond.com. Ice skating admission $6 for people 58" & taller; free for all others. Skate rentals $12 adults, $6 kids. Free access to spray pool in summer. Carousel $3, open mid-Apr through Oct.*

10 ★★ Brewer Fountain. The elaborate bronze fountain near the Park Street subway entrance is an exact replica of an installation at the 1855 Paris World's Fair. The reclining figures at the base are Poseidon and Amphitrite, Acis and Galatea. South of the fountain is a small **visitor center** (with a public bathroom). *www.friendsofthepublic garden.org.*

11 ★ Parkman Bandstand. The Classical Revival bandstand sits at the center of a network of paths surrounded by stately trees.

The amber-hued **12 ★ Explorateur,** a casual French cafe at the corner of Tremont and Boylston, is open for breakfast, lunch, dinner, and drinks. *186 Tremont St.* ☎ *617/466-6600. www.explorateur. com. $–$$.*

The Esplanade & Charles River

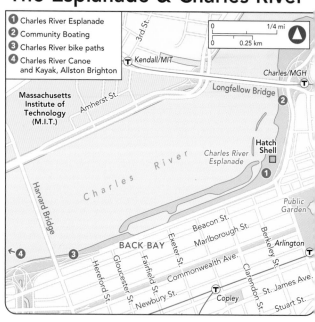

1 Charles River Esplanade
2 Community Boating
3 Charles River bike paths
4 Charles River Canoe and Kayak, Allston Brighton

Massachusetts Institute of Technology (M.I.T.)

Charles River Esplanade

Hatch Shell

BACK BAY

Public Garden

Beacon St.
Marlborough St.
Commonwealth Ave.
Newbury St.
Copley
Arlington
St. James Ave.
Stuart St.

For many Bostonians, the Esplanade along the Charles River is where we meet friends to go walking (or running, or biking, or skating). There are also plenty of options for getting out on to the water from here and further along the river. START: **Charles/ MGH T. Cross the footbridge over Storrow Drive.**

1 ★★ Charles River Esplanade. The Esplanade (say es-pluh-nod) along the Boston side of the Charles River is one of the city's busiest parks. Its 64 acres have paths for biking and running, and green spaces for picnicking and lounging under a tree. The **Hatch Shell** amphitheater is here, an Art Deco confection with a rustic terrazzo exterior—and if you arrive at the right time, you can plunk down on the lawn to listen to music for free (p 132). The narrow **Storrow Lagoon** has postcard-pretty footbridges at either end and is surrounded by

elaborate plantings and shady trees. Before landfill was used to build this park, the Charles River ended in a tidal basin rimmed with reeking mud flats, unpleasant to both eyes and noses, which is why the magnificent old residences on Beacon Street don't face the water. The major entrance is at the Charles/MGH T stop, although the park can be accessed by eight footbridges that cross over Storrow Drive, the highway that divides the city from the park and river. *From Charles River Dam Road (near the Museum of Science) to the Boston University Bridge*

The Hatch Shell is the site of public concerts, including Boston's July Fourth celebration.

(& beyond). www.esplanade association.org. T: Charles/MGH.

②ᐟ★ Community Boating. The Standells immortalized the Charles River with their 1966 "Dirty Water"—back when the river was a mess. Today it's cleaner and attracts lots of boaters. Near the entrance to the Esplanade from the Charles/MGH T stop is the Community Boating boathouse, where thousands of people have learned to sail. Experienced visitors can **rent sailboats, kayaks, and stand-up paddleboards** to take into the Charles River basin for the day. The basin is also where **Duck Boat tours** trundle into the water (p 30, **⑥**) if you'd rather be a passenger than a captain. *21 David G. Mugar Way.* ☎ *617/523-1038. www. community-boating.org.*

③ ★★ Charles River bike paths. Bike paths on both sides of the river go all the way to Watertown, a suburb 8½ miles northwest of Boston (and beyond, with new extensions). Both sides are busy with bike commuters, runners, and walkers, especially closest to the city. Find a good PDF map online: *www.mass.gov/eea/docs/dcr/parks/ charlesriver/map-chasbasin.pdf*

④ ★★ kids Charles River Canoe and Kayak, Allston Brighton. Four miles northwest of

the Esplanade, the Charles narrows. Views are particularly bucolic before and after the Anderson Memorial Bridge, which crosses the river a few blocks from Harvard Square. One mile beyond that bridge, on the south side of the river, **Paddle Boston** sets up each spring with rentals of water craft. The river has just a modest current here, making it a great place for an hour or two of paddling around. (More determined folks can rent here and head back toward Boston, dropping craft off at Paddle Boston's Kendall Square location near MIT.) The **Artesani Playground, Spray Deck & Wading Pool** is also in this stretch along the river, with a large, free parking lot. *1071 Soldiers Field Rd.* ☎ *617/965-5110. www. paddleboston.com. Most rentals $9–$25 an hour. Artesani: 1255 Soldiers Field Rd. www.mass.gov.*

A small lagoon along the Charles River Esplanade is crisscrossed by four small pedestrian bridges.

Whale Watches, Cruises & Boston Harbor Islands

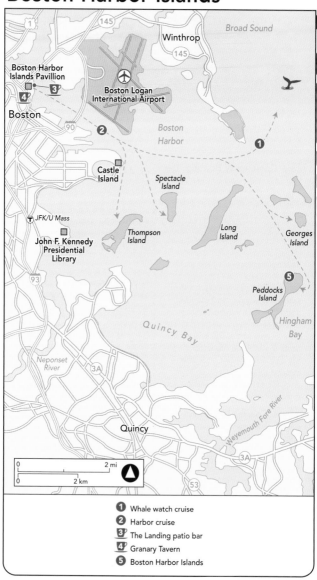

1 Whale watch cruise
2 Harbor cruise
3 The Landing patio bar
4 Granary Tavern
5 Boston Harbor Islands

It's easy and exhilarating to take to the ocean from downtown Boston. Cruises tour the city coastline and head to where whales frolic, just an hour off shore. Ferries take visitors to small, raw islands that speckle the harbor and house the remains of forts. There are also beautiful shoreline beaches 1 to 2 hours away by car that are good for swimming and getting some sand under your toes. START: **Aquarium T.**

Boston Harbor Cruises' specialty cruises focus on whales, history, the nighttime sky, and more.

1 ★★ **kids** **Whale watch cruise.** Straight east from Boston, in the Massachusetts Bay heading toward the Atlantic, is a large section of ocean designated as the **Stellwagen Bank Marine Sanctuary** (www.stellwagen.noaa.gov). Whales live here: humpback, finback, minke, pilot, and endangered right whales. Dolphins are here, too. Boat tours—usually 3 hours, sometimes longer depending on where the whales are—almost always have a sighting of these magnificent creatures, who often are curious and playful around the customized catamarans. Naturalists trained by the **New England Aquarium** (p 12, **10**) are aboard each trip. *One Long Wharf.* ☎ *617/ 227-4321. www.neaq.org/exhibits/ whale-watch. Tickets $53 adults & kids 12 & up, $45 seniors, $33 kids 3–11, $16 kids under 3. Discounted packages with Aquarium tickets available. Daily late March to mid Nov. Check website for times & frequency, which vary considerably throughout the season. T: Aquarium.*

2 ★★ **kids** **Harbor cruise.** Visiting the whales **1** in New England's waters is just one option for a harbor cruise. Others include a 90-minute **Historic Sightseeing Cruise,** a 45-minute **USS Constitution Cruise,** a 40-minute **Codzilla "high-speed thrill"** boat ride, a 90-minute **Sunset Cruise,** and a 3-hour nighttime **Sea the Stars Cruise,** produced in conjunction with the **Museum of Science** (p 31, **7**). Boats leave from the wharf next to the New England Aquarium. *One Long Wharf.* ☎ *617/227-4321. www. bostonharborcruises.com. Daily late Mar to mid Nov; check website for times & prices, which vary considerably throughout the season. T: Aquarium.*

Beaches for Ocean Swimming

There are great beaches for swimming within a 45- to 90-minute drive from downtown Boston. All have public parking and some add concessions. **Duxbury Beach** (www.duxburybeachpark.com) on the South Shore and **Plum Island** (www.newburyport.com/plum-island-beach) and **Cranes Beach** (www.thetrustees.org/places-to-visit/north-shore/crane-beach) on the North Shore are serene and beautiful. **Ogunquit Beach** (www.ogunquit.org) is a favorite, and although it's in Maine it's only 78 miles away. It has a long, sandy beach, seaside parking and concessions, an ocean cliff walk, and a sweet little town with restaurants, a candy shop, and a toy store. Because it attracts visitors from Québec, many of the signs are in both English and French.

For drinks (and Jell-O shots), **3** **The Landing patio bar** (p 116) is next to where the cruise boats dock. For something more substantial, **4** **Granary Tavern** just across the Rose Kennedy Greenway has sandwiches, salad, and fun options like chicken & waffles. *170 Milk St.* ☎ *617/449-7110. www.granarytavern.com. $–$$.*

5 ★★ kids **Boston Harbor Islands.** In the waters near South Boston, 34 islands ranging in size from small to miniscule make up the Boston Harbor Islands National and State Park. Six are publicly accessible by **ferry** and can be visited for day trips (a couple have campgrounds, too). Visiting the islands is a raw experience: limited concessions, limited toilet facilities, and limited shelter from sun or rain. That said, a visit can be an invigorating adventure and one of the most memorable ways to experience Boston. **Georges Island** has the historic **Fort Warren** to explore. It was built before the Civil War and was a prison for Confederate officers, and visitors can walk its dark corridors (and keep an eye out

for the **Lady in Black ghost**). There are paved and mostly level paths on Georges, and a snack bar that's open daily in summer. **Spectacle Island** is the highest point in the harbor and has spectacular views of Boston and the other harbor islands. It has 5 miles of trails and a swimming beach with lifeguards in summer, and a snack bar. **Peddocks Island** has **Fort Andrews,** an active coastal fort until it was decommissioned in 1946; Fort Andrew's brick barracks each housed over 100 soldiers, elegant officers' quarters, and a hospital. The **Boston Harbor Islands Pavilion and Welcome Center** is on the Rose Kennedy Greenway at 191 W. Atlantic Ave. (near Faneuil Hall Marketplace) and staffed by National Park Service rangers. *www.bostonharborislands.org. Ferries: One Long Wharf.* ☎ *617/227-4321. www.bostonharborcruises.com. Round-trip fares $17 adults, $12 seniors & students, $10 kids. Ferries depart from Long Wharf May–Oct. During the summer season, the trip to Georges is 40 min., the trip to Spectacle is 20 min. & the trip to Peddocks is 1 hr. Check the website for schedules. T: Aquarium.* ●

Dining Best Bets

Oysters at Durgin-Park, in Faneuil Hall Marketplace. Previous page: The classic New England lobster roll.

Best Seafood
★★★ Legal Sea Foods $$ 26 Park Plaza and branches (p 106)

Best Raw Bar
★★ Row 34 $$ 383 Congress St. (p 108)

Best Clam Shack
★ The Barking Crab $$ 88 Sleeper St. (p 102)

Best New American
★★★ Craigie On Main $$ 853 Main St., Cambridge (p 104)

Best French
★★★ L'Espalier $$$$ 774 Boylston St. (p 106)

Best Brasserie
★★ Brasserie JO $$ 120 Huntington Ave. (p 103)

Best Elegant Italian
★★★ Mamma Maria $$$$ 3 North Square (p 106)

Best Down-Home Italian
★ La Famiglia Giorgio $$ 112 Salem St. (p 106)

Best Spanish
★★ Toro $$ 1704 Washington St. (p 109)

Best Mediterranean
★★ Oleana $$$ 134 Hampshire St., Cambridge (p 107)

Best Barbecue
★★ Sweet Cheeks $$ 1381 Boylston St. (p 109)

Best Pub Food
★★ Grendel's Den Restaurant & Bar $ 89 Winthrop St., Cambridge (p 105)

Best Pizza
★ Regina Pizzeria $ 11½ Thacher St. (p 108)

Best Classic Dim Sum
★ Hei La Moon $ 88 Beach St. (p 105)

Best Fanciful Dim Sum
★★ Myers + Chang $$ 1145 Washington St. (p 107)

Best Vegetarian
★★ Clover Food Lab $ 1326 Mass. Ave., Cambridge and branches (p 103)

Best Salads
★★ Sweetgreen $ 659 Boylston St. and branches (p 109)

Best Bakery
★★ Flour Bakery + Cafe $ 12 Farnsworth St. and branches (p 104)

Cambridge Dining

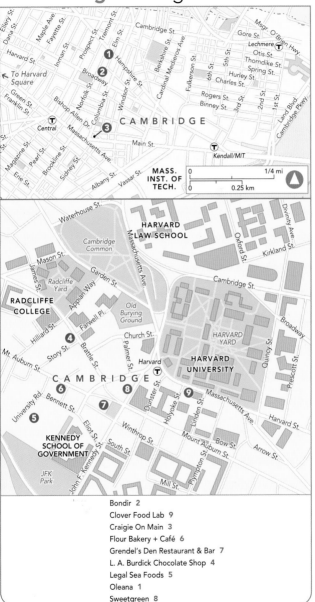

Bondir 2
Clover Food Lab 9
Craigie On Main 3
Flour Bakery + Café 6
Grendel's Den Restaurant & Bar 7
L. A. Burdick Chocolate Shop 4
Legal Sea Foods 5
Oleana 1
Sweetgreen 8

Boston Dining

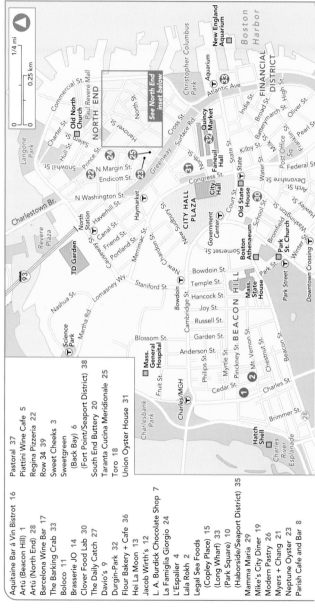

Aquitaine Bar á Vin Bistrot 16
Artú (Beacon Hill) 1
Artú (North End) 28
Barcelona Wine Bar 17
The Barking Crab 33
Boloco 11
Brasserie JO 14
Clover Food Lab 30
The Daily Catch 27
Davio's 9
Durgin-Park 32
Flour Bakery + Cafe 36
Hei La Moon 13
Jacob Wirth's 12
L. A. Burdick Chocolate Shop 7
La Famiglia Giorgio 24
L'Espalier 4
Lala Rokh 2
Legal Sea Foods
   (Copley Place) 15
   (Long Wharf) 33
   (Park Square) 10
   (Haborside/Seaport District) 35
Mamma Maria 29
Mike's City Diner 19
Modern Pastry 26
Myers + Chang 21
Neptune Oyster 23
Parish Cafe and Bar 8

Pastoral 37
Piattini Wine Cafe 5
Regina Pizzeria 22
Row 34 39
Sweet Cheeks 3
Sweetgreen
   (Back Bay) 6
   (Fort Point/Seaport District) 38
South End Buttery 20
Taranta Cucina Meridionale 25
Toro 18
Union Oyster House 31

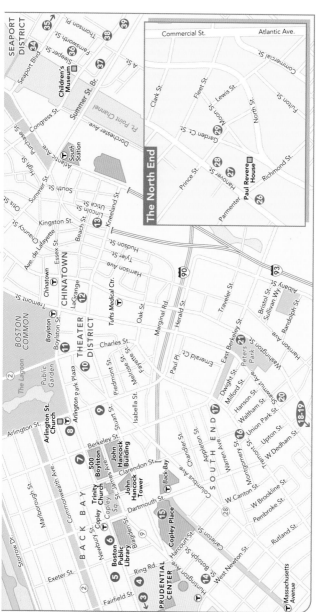

Dining A to Z

★★ **Aquitaine Bar á Vin Bistrot** SOUTH END *FRENCH* This nook of the South End is a destination for romantic brunches and dinners. Aquitaine, which has been holding court here since 1998, is part of the reason. The French bistro covers all the essential territory, with a luscious *soupe à l'oignon gratinée*, steak frites, and sole meuniere. Cassoulet is served on Sundays. *569 Tremont St.* ☎ *617/424-8577. www.aquitaineboston.com. Entrees $25–$38. Lunch & dinner daily. T: Back Bay & 10-min. walk. Map p 100.*

★ **kids Artú** NORTH END *ITALIAN* Right on the Freedom Trail in the heart of the Italian North End neighborhood, Artú is a neighborhood favorite with terrific pastas, sandwiches, and roasted meats. In addition to this location, there's an outpost on Beacon Hill, at 89 Charles St. *6 Prince St.* ☎ *617/742-4336. www.artuboston.com. Entrees $16–$35 (lunch $8–$17). Lunch & dinner daily. T: Haymarket. Map p 100.*

★★ **Barcelona Wine Bar** SOUTH END *SPANISH* The *Boston Globe* pegged the trendy Barcelona right when it said that the menu navigates a line "that threads tradition, invention, and ambition." Tapas offerings include both traditional standbys like *pan con tomate* (bread rubbed with tomato, garlic, and olive oil) and *mussels al ajillo* (mussels in garlic sauce) as well as unconventional concoctions such as crispy eggplant with smoked maple and pickled beets with pesto and feta. The atmosphere is festive and the restaurant is usually packed. *525 Tremont St.* ☎ *617/266-2600. www.barcelonawinebar.com. Tapas $5–$11. Dinner daily, brunch Sat–Sun.*

A small sampling of the tapas at Barcelona Wine Bar.

T: Back Bay & 10-min. walk. Map p 100.

★ **kids The Barking Crab** SEAPORT DISTRICT *SEAFOOD* New England's coastline is chock-a-block with clam shacks (where the seafood is deep fried) and lobster shacks (with deep pots of water to boil or steam lobsters). Guests often sit elbow to elbow at picnic tables and dig into lobster rolls, whole lobsters with butter, baskets piled high with fried clams, and sides like corn on the cob and potato salad. The Barking Crab offers all of that, right in the heart of the city. It's located on the Fort Point channel, qualifying it as a seaside restaurant. *88 Sleeper St.* ☎ *617/426-2722. www.barkingcrab.com. Entrees $12–$51. Lunch & dinner daily. T: Courthouse. Map p 100.*

★★ kids **Boloco** BACK BAY *BURRITOS* Tasty, consistent, and cheery, this Boston fast-casual chain (there are 7 locations in the city) is a dependable option for a quick, healthy meal. Burritos and bowls come in flavors such as Bangkok Thai (peanut sauce, Asian slaw, cucumbers, brown rice) and The Summer (mango salsa, melted cheese, black beans, rice), with a full range of protein options including chicken, steak, pork carnitas, and tofu. This location looks out onto the Boston Common. *176 Boylston St.* ☎ *617/778-6772. www. boloco.com. All items $9 or less. Breakfast, lunch & dinner daily. T: Boylston. Map p 100. Check the website for additional locations.*

★★★ **Bondir** CAMBRIDGE *NEW AMERICAN* Settling in for a dining experience at chef Jason Bond's luxuriously inventive restaurant is like visiting the dining room of a friend who happens to be an artisan gourmand: There are barely a dozen tables, rock music sets a casual mood, and a single $68 five-course menu (no à la carte options) means that you give yourself over to whatever the chef has planned for that evening. Menu descriptions

might include "Mangalitsa Pork Shoulder, Parsley Root, Hedgehog Mushrooms, Walnuts" or "Seared Mackerel with Foie Gras, Squash, Crosnes, Perigord Truffle Vinaigrette." *279A Broadway.* ☎ *617/661-0009. www.bondircambridge.com. 5-course dinner $68. Dinner Wed–Sun. T: Central Square & 10-min. walk. Map p 99.*

★★ kids **Brasserie JO** BACK BAY *FRENCH* A classic brasserie—with long hours (6:30am–midnight weekdays, 7am–midnight weekends) and a wide-ranging menu. Tarte flambée (or *flammekueche*), the Alsatian-style pizza, is a specialty here, and served both in its classic form (with onion, bacon, and fromage blanc, or *crème fraiche*) and with a few nifty combinations including salmon, capers, and egg. *120 Huntington Ave., in the Colonnade Hotel.* ☎ *617/424-7000. www. colonnadehotel.com/brasserie-jo. Entrees $18–$39. Breakfast, lunch & dinner daily. T: Back Bay. Map p 100.*

★★ kids **Clover Food Lab** CAMBRIDGE *VEGETARIAN/ VEGAN* Clover is a graduate of the food-truck scene: It started in 2008 with extremely popular trucks serving vegetarian and vegan fare

Good times at the Barking Crab.

to MIT students and staff (its founder is an MIT alum), and now has 12 brick-and-mortar locations throughout the Boston, Cambridge, and nearby suburbs. Standouts include its egg and eggplant sandwich, French fries with rosemary, and mezze platter of vegetables. Most locations include an appealing selection of iced teas and local beers. *1326 Mass. Ave. www.clover foodlab.com. All items $9 or less. Breakfast, lunch & dinner daily. T: Harvard. Map p 99. Also at 27 School St. on the Freedom Trail, Park Street T. Check the website for additional locations.*

★★★ **Craigie On Main** CAMBRIDGE *NEW AMERICAN*   Both polished and rustic, Craigie is one of the city's top restaurants for special meals. The five- and seven-course tasting menus ($85 and $108) provide a chance to sit back and try plate after innovate plate of seasonal fare. Chef Tony Maws also hosts inventive special events, including chef's whim Sundays, burger and beer lunches with Somerville brewery Aeronaut, and a comfy Passover meal with matzoh ball soup and asparagus with chicken liver sauce. *853 Main St. ☎ 617/497-5511. www.craigieon main.com. Tasting menus $85 & $108; 3-course prix fixe $65; entrees $35. Dinner Tues–Sun; brunch Sun. T: Central. Map p 99.*

★ **The Daily Catch** NORTH END *SEAFOOD/SOUTHERN ITALIAN* Follow the aroma of garlic to this tiny storefront (just 20 seats). The lines are long, the specialty is calamari (squid), and everything is delicious. *323 Hanover St. ☎ 617/ 523-8567. www.thedailycatch.com. Entrees $16–$30. Cash only. Lunch & dinner daily. T: Haymarket. Map p 100.*

★★ **Davio's** BACK BAY *NORTHERN ITALIAN/STEAK* Steakhouse favorites and inventive starters like Philly cheesesteak spring rolls share the menu with Northern Italian classics, including a sumptuous lobster risotto. Somehow, it works beautifully. *75 Arlington St. ☎ 617/357-4810. www.davios.com. Entrees $20–$59 Lunch weekdays, brunch Sun, dinner daily. T: Arlington. Map p 100.*

★★ kids **Durgin-Park** FANEUIL HALL MARKETPLACE *NEW ENGLAND*   A true old-timey Boston landmark, with the tagline "Established before you were born." Durgin-Park serves up classic New England fare: Boston baked beans, chicken pot pie, Yankee pot roast, prime rib, boiled scrod, and a full New England Clambake (clam chowder, steamers, lobster, boiled potato, and corn on the cob). Long communal tables with red and white checked tablecloths give the dining rooms a boardinghouse feel, but they're not terribly noisy and the overall ambiance is warm and convivial. *340 Faneuil Hall Marketplace ☎ 617/227-2038. www.ark restaurants.com/durgin_park. Entrees $13–$35. Lunch & dinner daily. T: Government Center. Map p 100.*

★★ kids **Flour Bakery + Cafe** FORT POINT/SEAPORT DISTRICT *BAKERY*   Chef/owner Joanne Chang is a Boston superstar, known for her small chain of high-end bakeries. (She's also the Chang in **Myers + Chang**, p 107.) Flour's sticky buns, made with caramel and pecan, are justifiably renowned, and sandwiches are also first-rate. There are also locations downtown and in Harvard Square. *12 Farnsworth St. ☎ 617/338-4333. www. flourbakery.com Baked goods $4–$6, sandwiches $8–$10. Breakfast, lunch & (early) dinner daily. T: Courthouse. Map p 99 & 100. Check the website for additional locations.*

★★ **kids** **Grendel's Den Restaurant & Bar** CAMBRIDGE *AMERICAN* With a faux fireplace and elbow-to-elbow tables, Grendel's, which has been around forever, is a friendly, popular college pub. The food is good—spinach pie, quinoa stew, portobello Reuben, burgers, and the like—and there's a daily lunch special for $6. Plus, every day from 5–7:30pm, all food is half price with the purchase of a $4 drink (consider the Paulaner Weissbier). In warm weather, a few tables are available on an appealing terrace. Open daily until 1am. *89 Winthrop St.* ☎ *617/491-1160. www.grendelsden. com. Entrees $8–$16. Lunch & dinner daily. T: Harvard. Map p 99.*

★ **kids** **Hei La Moon** CHINATOWN *DIM SUM/CHINESE* A gigantic banquet hall with a sea of red and gold tables brings in crowds, especially on the weekend. The highlight here is dim sum, available daily. If it's your first time, start with Shrimp Har Gao (shrimp dumplings) or Char Siu Bao (steamed barbeque pork buns). The restaurant is on the section of Beach Street closest to South Station, and there's a parking lot *above* the restaurant. *88 Beach St.*

☎ *617/338-8813. Entrees $8–$13. Dim sum, lunch & dinner daily. T: South Station. Map p 100.*

★ **Jacob Wirth** THEATER DISTRICT *GERMAN* The decor suggests cavernous Munich beer hall, and rib-sticking specialties include wursts and Wiener schnitzel. On Thursday, Friday, and Saturday nights there's a rousing piano-led sing-a-long, which grows ever more boisterous as the night wears on. The restaurant was for sale at the time of writing, so check ahead. *31–37 Stuart St.* ☎ *617/338-8586. www.jacobwirth.com. Entrees $10–$24. Lunch & dinner daily. T: Boylston. Map p 100.*

★★ **kids** **L. A. Burdick Chocolate Shop** BACK BAY *CAFE* Cute and cozy, this little cafe—tucked inside a teeny house next to a skyscraper—serves hot and iced chocolate, coffee and tea, and luscious pastries. It's also a retail location for the New Hampshire–based luxury chocolatier's dreamy confections, which include its signature chocolate mice. *220 Clarendon St.* ☎ *617/303-0113. www.burdickchocolate. com. About $10 for a drink & a pastry. Breakfast, lunch & dinner daily. T: Arlington. Map p 99 & 100.*

Jacob Wirth has served German fare in the Theater District since 1868.

★ kids La Famiglia Giorgio

NORTH END *ITALIAN* You want your red sauce? Or maybe an Alfredo or bolognese or puttanesca? You want your bruschetta and garlic bread, your *pasta fagioli* and fried calamari, your fettuccini, lasagna, and spaghetti and meatballs? You want your gigantic portions and reasonable prices? You want your old-fashioned family atmosphere, the kind you imagine if you're not Italian? You're looking for Giorgio's. Gluten-free pasta is even available. *112 Salem St.* ☎ *617/367-6711. www.lafamiglia giorgios.com. Entrees $10–$23. Lunch & dinner daily. T: Haymarket. Map p 100.*

★ Lala Rokh

BEACON HILL *PERSIAN* Boston's premiere Iranian restaurant, tucked into a side street on swanky Beacon Hill, was freshened up a few years ago with some contemporary touches, including leather-lined banquettes and long bar to dine at. But its offerings remain traditional and elegant: lamb medallions, ground beef *Kubideh* with aromatic Persian spice, and cardamom- and rosewater-poached pears to end the meal. *97 Mt Vernon St.* ☎ *617/720-5511. www.lalarokh. com. Entrees $19–$25. Dinner daily. T: Charles/MGH. Map p 100.*

★★★ kids Legal Sea Foods

BACK BAY *SEAFOOD* The city's reigning seafood chain has over a dozen outposts in the area, counting the airport and nearby Cambridge. Its food is uniformly excellent, from starters like oysters and clam chowder and crab cakes to full-on seafood entrees. There's a long dessert menu, but why look farther than Boston cream pie, perhaps paired with a nice tawny port? When in Rome. . . . Check the website for locations; three prominent ones are listed here. *26 Park Plaza.* ☎ *617/426-4444. www.legalseafoods.com.* *Entrees $17–$36. Lunch & dinner daily. T: Arlington. Also in Copley Place mall, 100 Huntington Ave.* ☎ *617/266-7775, T: Back Bay; & in the Seaport District at a massive venue at 270 Northern Ave.,* ☎ *617/ 477-2900, T: Silver Line Way. Map p 99 & 100.*

★★★ L'Espalier

BACK BAY *FRENCH* Boston's most esteemed white tablecloth restaurant is elegant, elaborate, and romantic. This is the place to pull out the stops for a special occasion. Inventive tasting menus are featured, but guests can mix and match from anything available that day to create their own menu. As befits a *haute cuisine* French restaurant, there is a lavish cheese selection. After years in an intimate Boston town house, the restaurant is now located inside the Mandarin Oriental hotel. *774 Boylston St.* ☎ *617/262-3023. www.lespalier.com. Three tasting menus at dinner: $98, $180, $285. Lunch & dinner daily, afternoon tea Sat–Sun. T: Copley. Map p 100.*

★★★ Mamma Maria

NORTH END *NORTHERN ITALIAN* Creative cuisine in an elegant town house at one of the most romantic squares in the city. Many come specifically for the veal shank osso buco served with saffron risotto Milanese. *3 North Square.* ☎ *617/523-0077. www.mammamaria.com. Entrees $27–$48. Dinner daily. T: Haymarket. Map p 100.*

★★ kids Mike's City Diner

SOUTH END *BREAKFAST* A neighborhood stalwart, Mike's serves huge portions of breakfast classics—eggs, buttermilk pancakes, breakfast burritos—plus hearty Reubens, Philly steak, and fried chicken. *1714 Washington St.* ☎ *617/267-9393. www.mikescity diner.com. Entrees $4–$14. Cash only. Breakfast & lunch daily. T: Worcester St. Map p 100.*

★★ Kids Modern Pastry NORTH
END *BAKERY* Cannoli—flaky,
deep-fried, filled with sweet ricotta
cream—are a specialty of the North
End Italian neighborhood. And just
as Montréal has a bagel war over
which of its great bagel shops is
best, there's a minor cannoli battle
here between the Modern and
Mike's Pastry, across the street at
300 Hanover (☎ 617/742-3050). It's
a little too tidy to say *tourists go to
Mike's, locals go to the Modern*
since both are terrific options for an
espresso and cannoli if you can
snag a seat (most people get their
pastries to go). On the other hand,
if you get your hankering at 2am,
there's only one option: **Bova's,** a
4-minute walk away at 134 Salem
St. (☎ 617/523-5601) It's open 24
hours, 7 days a week—and some
swear Bova's cannoli are best. *257
Hanover St.* ☎ *617/523-3783. www.
modernpastry.com. Cannoli $3.50.
Daily 8am–10pm (11pm on Fri, midnight on Sat). T: Haymarket. Map
p 100.*

★★ Myers + Chang SOUTH
END *ASIAN FUSION* Inspired by
Southeast Asian street food, this
stylish restaurant has small-plate
menu items bundled into categories such as "dim sum-y things" and
"buns, baos, rolls + a taco." It's a
good place to come with a few
people so that you can order a
mountain of food to try. *1145 Washington St.* ☎ *617/542-5200. www.
myersandchang.com. Entrees $14–
$29, small plates $5–$17. Lunch &
dinner daily, dim sum brunch Sat–
Sun. T: Washington St. @ Herald St.
Map p 100.*

★★ Neptune Oyster NORTH
END *SEAFOOD* Tiny and
crammed, and with a line often
extending down the block, Neptune is an open secret: The busy little kitchen produces some of the
best seafood in the city. High-end

lobster rolls, fried clams, and, of
course, oysters all get raves. There
are burgers, too—served with fried
oysters and garlic mayo. *63 Salem
St.* ☎ *617/742-3474. www.neptune
oyster.com. Entrees $21–$39. Lunch
& dinner daily. T: Haymarket. Map
p 100.*

★★ Oleana CAMBRIDGE *MEDI-
TERRANEAN* Emphatic Middle
Eastern flavors, seasonal ingredients, and a cozy atmosphere give
longtime Oleana its deserved status as a top Cambridge go-to. In
cold weather its moussaka—made
with smoky eggplant puree, crispy
cauliflower, and mint—and its
lemon chicken with *za'atar* spice
are a shot of summer. Don't miss
executive pastry chef Maura Kilpat-
rick's baked Alaska with coconut ice
cream and passion fruit caramel. In
good weather, there's a delightful
patio. Star chef Ana Sortun has
opened similar Turkish-tinged venues in recent years, including the
always packed **Sofra Bakery and
Café,** a mile and a half west of
Harvard Square at 1 Belmont St.
(☎ 617/661-3161) also in Cambridge. *134 Hampshire St.* ☎ *617/
661-0505. www.oleanarestaurant.
com. Entrees $26–$30. Dinner daily.
T: Central, 10-min. walk. Map p 99.*

★★ Parish Cafe and Bar BACK
BAY *AMERICAN* The conceit here
is clever: Ask some of Boston's star
chefs for a sandwich recipe, then
put them all onto one menu. Parish
Cafe has made it work for over 25
years, providing guests sneak peeks
into the flavor profiles of restaurants all over the city. The menu has
been updated in recent years, but
it's kept a long-time favorite: the
Zuni Roll, by Norma Gillaspie:
smoked turkey, bacon, scallions, dill
Havarti cheese, and cranberry chipotle sauce in a warm tortilla with a
side of sour cream. The restaurant
is busy with the office crowd at

lunch and after work for drinks. The kitchen serves the full menu until 1am. *361 Boylston St.* ☎ *617/247-4777. www.parishcafe.com. Sandwiches & entrees $10–$20. Lunch & dinner daily. T: Arlington. Map p 100.*

★★ kids Pastoral FORT POINT/ SEAPORT DISTRICT PIZZA

With artisan pizza, a roomy main restaurant, and a hopping bar with a wide selection of U.S. and Italian wines and craft beers, Pastoral comfortably accommodates both the nearby work crowd and families who have just come out of the Boston Children's Museum down the block. *345 Congress St.* ☎ *617/345-0005. www.pastoralfortpoint.com. Entrees $11–$22. Lunch & dinner daily. T: Courthouse. Map p 100.*

★★ Piattini Wine Cafe BACK BAY ITALIAN

Great value on the Newbury Street shopping mecca, especially at lunch, where the hearty pasta, panini, and pizzas are all $8 to $14, with most priced right at $10—including the spinach gnocchi with pesto cream sauce, the homemade fusilli with bolognese sauce, and the chicken Parm panini. There's an outside patio in good weather. *226 Newbury St.* ☎ *617/536-2020. www. piattini.com. Entrees $16–$28. Lunch & dinner daily. T: Copley. Map p 100.*

★ kids Regina Pizzeria NORTH END PIZZA

That picture you have in your head of a neighborhood pizza place in an old-time Italian neighborhood? This is it. Regina Pizzeria is a true Boston classic (founded in 1926), on an atmospheric corner

of the city's still-traditional Italian neighborhood. There are 14 outlets throughout the city and region, but this is the original—an obvious choice if you're walking the Freedom Trail. *11½ Thacher St.* ☎ *617/227-0765. www.pizzeriaregina.com. Pizza $10–$21. Lunch & dinner daily. T: Haymarket. Map p 100.*

★★ Row 34 SEAPORT DISTRICT SEAFOOD

With a short menu—dominated by oysters, crudo, and ceviche, and including a handful of fish dishes and one or two chicken and beef choices—as well as a long list of wine options and an upscale industrial vibe, Row 34 is at the vanguard of the Seaport District's renaissance. It represents what's both new and classic about this hot neighborhood. *383 Congress St.* ☎ *617/553-5900. www.row34.com. Entrees $16–$29. Lunch & dinner daily. T: Courthouse. Map p 100.*

★★ kids South End Buttery SOUTH END CONTEMPORARY AMERICAN

Boston's South End is rife with cozy spots for brunch, dinner, and drinks, and few are more appealing than the Buttery. Its small cafe is open from 6am to 6pm, and the attached bar and restaurant are open nightly for dinner and on weekends for brunch. If you are in need of some decadent comfort food, the macaroni and cheese comes with steamed lobster tails and claws. The Buttery also has a cafe/ market with a few seats at 37 Clarendon St. (☎ 617/482-1015), also in the South End; it's

The original Regina Pizza is tucked into an atmospheric corner of the North End.

open daily from 6:30am to 6pm.
314 Shawmut Ave. ☎ *617/482-1015.*
www.southendbuttery.com. Entrees
$18–$25. Dinner daily; brunch Sat–
Sun; breakfast & lunch in cafe only
daily. T: Washington St. @ Union Pk.
Map p 100.

★★ **Sweet Cheeks** FENWAY
BARBECUE Casual, big, and loud,
this upscale joint near Fenway Park
features chef Tiffani Faison's succu-
lent barbecue, hospitable service,
and Southern buttermilk biscuits
that are so popular that the restaurant added a breakfast grab-and-go
option and sell them all day long.
1381 Boylston St. ☎ *617/266-1300.*
www.sweetcheeksq.com. Entrees
$11–$26. Lunch & dinner daily &
breakfast take-out. T: Fenway. Map
p 100.

★★ **Sweetgreen** BACK BAY
LIGHT FARE The "salad-as-star"
trend is a welcome one, and purveyor Sweetgreen has taken Boston's lunch crowds by storm with its
healthy and hearty salads and grain
bowls. Dishes are made to order
and tossed in a big bowl, making it
easy to dig right into. Kale Caesar
salad and the Harvest Bowl—with
kale, apples, sweet potatoes,
roasted chicken, goat cheese, and
toasted almonds—are popular
standbys. *659 Boylston St.* ☎ *617/*
936-3464. www.sweetgreen.com.
Entrees $9–$12. Lunch & dinner daily.
T: Copley. Map p 99 & 100. Check
the website for additional locations.

★★ **Taranta Cucina Meridio-**
nale NORTH END *ITALIAN/*
PERUVIAN The flavors of the
owner-chef's native Peru jazz up
Taranta's menu, which deftly combines neighborhood favorites and
culinary adventure. *210 Hanover St.*
☎ *617/720-0052. www.tarantarist.*
com. Entrees $19–$39. Dinner daily.
T: Haymarket. Map p 100.

Plenty of Boston restaurants serve fresh
seafood. Try Row 34 or Neptune Oyster
for some of the best. Union Oyster
House serves it with a side of history.

★★ **Toro** SOUTH END *SPANISH*
The draw here is authentic tapas.
Guests usually choose 2 to 3 small
plates each to share with the table.
Toro's *maíz asado* (grilled corn on
the cob with aioli, lime, Espelette
pepper, and aged cheese) is justifiably one of the top dishes in Boston. Other menu favorites include
pimentos del Padron (spicy fried
green peppers), *chorizo Iberico de*
Fermin (Spanish pork sausage), and
gambas al ajillo (garlic shrimp with
chilies). Toro is just busy enough at
lunch, and noisy, fun, and packed at
dinner. *1704 Washington St.* ☎ *617/*
536-4300. www.toro-restaurant.com.
Tapas $5–$16. Lunch weekdays, din-
ner daily & brunch Sun. T: Worcester
Sq. Map p 100.

★ **kids Union Oyster House**
FANEUIL HALL MARKETPLACE
SEAFOOD The country's oldest

Sweet Cheeks is famous for its barbeque and buttermilk biscuits.

restaurant (since 1826) is on the Freedom Trail and gets enough tourists to justify a gift shop. The food is pricey—you're paying for *ye olde* atmosphere—but the chowders and oyster options get consistently good marks. John F. Kennedy apparently was a regular, and the upstairs dining room has a dedicated "Kennedy Booth" at the spot the restaurant says was his favorite. *41 Union St.* ☎ *617/227-2750. www. unionoysterhouse.com. Entrees $22–$39. Lunch & dinner daily. T: Haymarket. Map p 100.* ●

Nightlife Best Bets

Top of the Hub is a perfect spot to soak in the skyline. Previous page: Fenway's House of Blues.

Best **Martini Bar**
★★★ Drink, *348 Congress St. (p 116)*

Best **Unexpected Bar**
★★ Bleacher Bar, *82A Lansdowne St. (p 120)*

Best **Fancy Hotel Bar**
★★ Oak Long Bar + Kitchen, in Fairmont Copley Plaza, *138 St. James Ave. (p 117)*

Best **Rooftop Bar**
★★ Legal Harborside, *270 Northern Ave., on Liberty Wharf (p 117)*

Best **Sports Bar**
★★ The Fours, *166 Canal St. (p 120)*

Best **Irish Pub**
★★ Mr. Dooley's Boston Tavern, *77 Broad St. (p 117)*

Best **Geek Pub**
★★ Meadhall, *90 Broadway / 4 Cambridge Center, Cambridge (p 117)*

Best **LBGTQ Scene**
★★ Club Café, *209 Columbus Ave. (p 119)*

Best **Sit-Down Music Club**
★★ City Winery Boston, *80 Beverly St. (p 119)*

Best **Rock Club**
★★★ The Sinclair, *52 Church St., Cambridge (p 120)*

Best **Folk Club**
★★ Club Passim, *47 Palmer St., Cambridge (p 119)*

Best **Old-School Jazz Club**
★ Wally's Cafe, *427 Massachusetts Ave. (p 119)*

Best **Upscale Jazz Club**
★★ Regattabar, *in The Charles Hotel, 1 Bennett St., Cambridge (p 118)*

Best **Comedy Club**
★ Laugh Boston, *425 Summer St. (p 118)*

Cambridge Nightlife

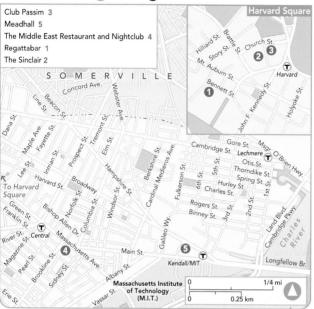

Club Passim 3
Meadhall 5
The Middle East Restaurant and Nightclub 4
Regattabar 1
The Sinclair 2

Seaport Nightlife

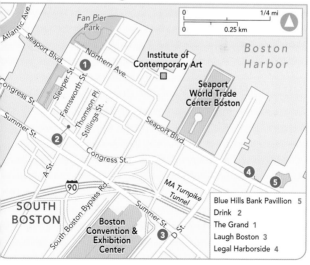

Blue Hills Bank Pavillion 5
Drink 2
The Grand 1
Laugh Boston 3
Legal Harborside 4

Boston Nightlife

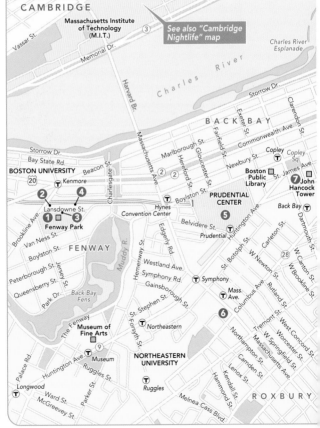

See also "Cambridge Nightlife" map

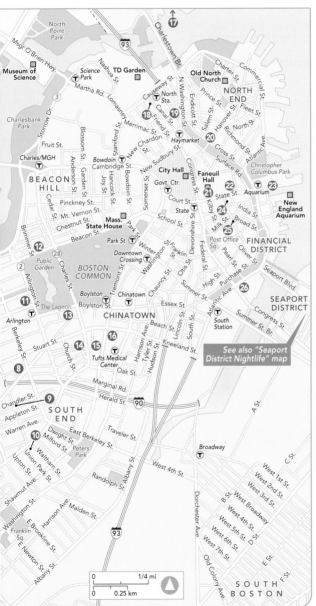

North Point Park

Msgr. O'Brien Hwy.

Museum of Science

Science Park Ⓣ

TD Garden

Nashua St.

Martha Rd.

Lomasney Way

Storrow Dr.

Charlesbank Park

Fruit St.

Charles/MGH Ⓣ

BEACON HILL

Blossom St.

Garden St.

Anderson St.

Stanford St.

Grove St.

Joy St.

Hancock St.

Bowdoin St.

Somerset St.

Pinckney St.

Mt. Vernon St.

Chestnut St.

Mass. State House

Beacon St.

Park St. Ⓣ

New Chardon St.

Bowdoin Ⓣ Cambridge St.

New Sudbury St.

City Hall

Govt. Ctr. Ⓣ

Court St.

State

School St.

Franklin St.

Winter St.

Washington St.

Chauncy St.

Summer St.

Charlestown Br.

⑰

I-93

Causeway St.

North Sta. Ⓣ

⑱

Canal St.

Friend St.

Merrimac St.

Haymarket Ⓣ

⑲

N. Washington St.

Endicott St.

Charter St.

Commercial St.

Old North Church

NORTH END

Prince St.

Salem St.

Hanover St.

Fleet St.

North St.

Richmond St.

Cross St.

Surface Rd.

⑳

Atlantic Ave.

Christopher Columbus Park

Aquarium Ⓣ

㉓

New England Aquarium

State St. Ⓣ

㉒

Congress St.

Faneuil Hall

㉑

Kilby St.

India St.

Broad St.

㉔

Milk St.

Post Office Sq.

㉕

Devonshire St.

Federal St.

High St.

Pearl St.

Oliver St.

Purchase St.

FINANCIAL DISTRICT

Seaport Blvd.

Brimmer St.

Public Garden

⑫

Charles St.

Arlington St.

⑪

Ⓣ

Arlington

The Lagoon

⑬

Boylston St.

Boylston Ⓣ

BOSTON COMMON

Tremont St.

Downtown Crossing Ⓣ

Chinatown Ⓣ

CHINATOWN

Essex St.

Beach St.

⑯

⑮

⑭

Tufts Medical Center Ⓣ

Oak St.

Harrison Ave.

Tyler St.

Hudson St.

Lincoln St.

Kneeland St.

South St.

South Station Ⓣ

Atlantic Ave.

Congress St.

Summer St.

Summer St. Br.

㉖

SEAPORT DISTRICT

See also "Seaport District Nightlife" map

Berkeley St.

⑧

Stuart St.

Church St.

Chandler St.

⑨

Appleton St.

Warren Ave.

⑩

Dwight St.

Milford St.

Waltham St.

Union Park St.

Upton St.

Shawmut Ave.

Washington St.

Harrison Ave.

Malden St.

Franklin Sq.

E. Brookline St.

E. Newton St.

Albany St.

SOUTH END

East Berkeley St.

Peters Park

Marginal Rd.

Herald St.

I-90

Traveler St.

West 4th St.

Randolph St.

Albany St.

Dorchester Ave.

I-93

Broadway Ⓣ

A St.

West 1st St.

West 2nd St.

West 3rd St.

West Broadway

B St.

West 4th St.

C St.

West 5th St.

D St.

West 6th St.

West 7th St.

E St.

F St.

Old Colony Ave.

SOUTH BOSTON

0   1/4 mi

0   0.25 km

Nightlife A to Z

Bars, Pubs & Lounges

★★ The Bar at Taj Boston
BACK BAY Elegant and old world, this lounge—in what started as a Ritz Carlton in 1926—has a baronial fireplace and a million-dollar view of the Boston Public Garden. There's a long menu of cocktails, wines, scotches, appetizers, and desserts. *In the Taj Boston, 15 Arlington St.* ☎ *617/598-5255. T: Arlington. Map p 114.*

★ The Black Rose
FANEUIL HALL MARKETPLACE A location just around the corner from Faneuil Hall Marketplace ensures that there's always a full house in this Irish pub for food, drink, and the Irish musicians who settle in at 9:30pm, 7 nights a week (and at 4pm on Sat and Sun). Locals and tourists join in the singing for convivial, blurry nights. Those who can't get enough can come back for breakfast (Sat and Sun). *160 State St.* ☎ *617/742-2286. www. blackroseboston.com. Cover $3–$10. T: Aquarium. Map p 114.*

★★ Bristol Bar
BACK BAY The posh bar in the Four Seasons is a magnet for a well-heeled older crowd and the perfect place for a martini or glass of wine. A menu of 18 kinds of "bar bites" is available (until 11:30pm Sun–Thurs and 12:30am Fri–Sat). *In the Four Seasons Hotel, 200 Boylston St.* ☎ *617/338-4400. www.fourseasons.com/boston. T: Arlington. Map p 114.*

★ Cheers
BEACON HILL & QUINCY MARKET The Beacon Hill bar whose exterior is featured in the opening credits of the TV show *Cheers* used to be called the Bull & Finch. Now it's called Cheers. The outside looks the same—many visitors pose for a photo right here—although the interior is nothing like the show. The "replica" Cheers in Quincy Market at the Faneuil Hall Marketplace looks a lot more like the set, and also has outdoor seating. *84 Beacon St.* ☎ *617/227-9605. www.cheersboston.com. T: Arlington. Map p 114. Also at Quincy Market,* ☎ *617/227-0150. T: Government Center. Map p 114.*

★ Delux Cafe
SOUTH END With a kitschy decor (a shrine to Elvis, a sparkly sculpture of Schlitz cans), good burgers and fish, and local microbrews, the Delux is friendly hipster bar. Year-round Christmas lights give it a festive glow. *100 Chandler St.* ☎ *617/338-5258. T: Back Bay. Map p 114.*

★★★ Drink
SEAPORT DISTRICT Come here for the best martinis. The location, in the downstairs of an industrial warehouse with street-level windows, feels both old fashioned and extremely modern. A small menu of food options is available from 4 to 11:30pm. The bar is part of the family of restaurants by local star Barbara Lynch, and if you're still hungry two of them are steps away: The more relaxed **Sportello** is just upstairs, and fancy **Menton** is right next door at 352 Congress. *348 Congress St.* ☎ *617/695-1806. www.drinkfortpoint.com T: Courthouse. Map p 113.*

★ Frenchie Wine Bistro
SOUTH END New in 2017, the Parisian-styled Frenchie has a few sidewalk tables and an appealing greenhouse. Many guests come for the "frosé," a rosé slushy. *560 Tremont St.* ☎ *857/233-5941. www.frenchie boston.com T: Back Bay. Map p 114.*

★ The Landing
WATERFRONT If drinking a neon-colored concoction out of a fish bowl is your thing,

Bristol Bar in the Four Seasons has bar bites late into the evenings.

then the Landing is your place. It's a large outdoor patio bar on Long Wharf, directly on the Boston harbor (open seasonally, 10am–11pm daily in good weather). It's managed by the Boston Harbor Cruise company, so lots of its patrons are going to or coming off boat trips. *1 Long Wharf.* ☎ *617/227-4321. www.boston harborcruises.com/the-landing. T: Aquarium. Map p 114.*

★★ **Legal Harborside** SEAPORT DISTRICT What a view! The enormous rooftop bar of a 3-floor complex of the **Legal Sea Foods** (p 106) chain looks out directly over the Boston Harbor. It attracts waves of bar-hoppers, especially on warm summer nights. Retractable glass walls and ceiling allow the bar to be enclosed in cold months and fully exposed in summer. *270 Northern Ave., on Liberty Wharf.* ☎ *617/ 477-2900. www.legalseafoods.com/ restaurants/boston-legal-harborside-floor-3-40. T: Courthouse. Map p 113.*

★★ **Meadhall** CAMBRIDGE The southeastern corner of Cambridge is home to MIT and tech companies launched by its grads, and both Google and Amazon also have offices here. Hard-working geeks play hard at Meadhall,

a cavernous, upscale gastropub offering more types of beers than anyone could try in a month. *90 Broadway / 4 Cambridge Center.* ☎ *617/714-4372. www.themeadhall. com. T: Kendall/MIT. Map p 113.*

★★ **Mr. Dooley's Boston Tavern** FINANCIAL DISTRICT Far enough off the tourist track to be a favorite with local office workers and homesick expats, Dooley's is an authentically decorated Irish pub. There's live music nightly and a menu that includes shepherd's pie, hot corned beef, and fish and chips. *77 Broad St.* ☎ *617/338-5656. www.mrdooleys.com. T: Aquarium. Map p 114.*

★★ **Oak Long Bar + Kitchen** BACK BAY Voted Best Hotel Bar in 2017 by *Boston* magazine readers, the bar within Fairmont Copley Plaza is an elegant establishment that serves food and drink from early morning to late evening. *In the Fairmont Copley Plaza Hotel, 138 St. James Ave.* ☎ *617/585-7222. www.oaklongbarkitchen.com. T: Copley. Map p 114.*

★ **Tiki Rock** FANEUIL HALL MARKETPLACE New in 2018, this tiki cocktail bar comes with a solid pedigree, with menus designed by chefs from top restaurants including **The Buttery** (p 108). The cocktail menu highlights old-timey favorites such as the Mai Tai and Painkiller— a rum, pineapple, coconut, and orange concoction that comes in a bowl and serves four. *2 Broad St.* ☎ *617/670-2222. www.tikirock.com. T: Aquarium. Map p 114.*

★★ **Trade** WATERFRONT Come for the bar scene, stay for the delectable, shareable flatbreads, small plates, and Mediterranean vegetable sides. *540 Atlantic Ave.* ☎ *617/451-1234. www.trade-boston.com. Menu items $10–$31. T: South Station. Map p 114.*

Casino

★ **Boston Harbor Casino** EVERETT After years of contentious debate, Massachusetts voted to allow casino gambling in the state. A major casino development by Wynn Resorts was scheduled to open summer of 2019 in Everett, a city north of Boston across the Mystic River from Charlestown. The plan includes 671 hotel rooms, waterfront dining, and new boat connections to downtown Boston. But after the 2018 resignation of Wynn CEO Steve Wynn following reports of sexual misconduct, the project's future was thrown into disarray. *www.wynn bostonharbor.com. Map p 114.*

Comedy Clubs

★★ **Improv Asylum** NORTH END With shows 7 days a week—and 4 on Saturday—Improv Asylum is always hopping. Given its location close to Faneuil Hall Marketplace and on the main drag of the tourist-heavy North End, most shows sell out, so get tickets in advance. *216 Hanover St. ☎ 617/263-6887. www.improvasylum.com. Tickets $7–$33. T: Haymarket. Map p 114.*

★ **Laugh Boston** SEAPORT DISTRICT Midsized (about 300 seats), and dedicated to stand up, Laugh Boston has performances 4 or 5 nights a week and special events such as Dirty Disney and the storytelling program The Moth. It's located inside the Westin Hotel. *425 Summer St. ☎ 617/725-2844. www.laughboston.com. Tickets $20–$35. T: World Trade Center. Map p 113.*

★★ **Wilbur Theatre** THEATER DISTRICT This historic theater—built in 1914 and lavishly renovated in 2008—is Boston's highest-profile comedy venue, bringing in big-names such as Trevor Noah, Maria Bamford, and Jim Jefferies. The space also books musical acts (Wyclef Jean, Blood, Sweat & Tears) when national and local comics aren't in the spotlight. *246 Tremont St. ☎ 617/248-9700. www.the wilburtheatre.com. Tickets $25–$200. T: Boylston. Map p 114.*

Dance Clubs

★ **The Grand** SEAPORT DISTRICT New in 2017, this dance club on the third floor of the Scorpion Bar is flashy, although as is often typical in these places the women look fabulous and the men have to be reminded not to wear ripped jeans. *58 Seaport Blvd. ☎ 617/322-0200. www.thegrandboston.com. $30 & way up. T: Courthouse. Map p 113.*

★ **Royale** THEATER DISTRICT A former hotel ballroom with a stage and a balcony, Royale books concerts, burlesque shows, and DJs. *279 Tremont St. ☎ 617/338-7699. www.royaleboston.com. Most dance nights & concerts free to $28. T: Boylston. Map p 114.*

Jazz Clubs

★★ **Regattabar** CAMBRIDGE An elegant venue in Harvard Square's posh **Charles Hotel** (p 138), the 220-seat Regattabar is an appealing locale for music and drinks. Booked by NYC's Blue Note Jazz Club, the schedule can be sporadic—sometimes just a half dozen shows in a month—so check the calendar. In summer, the club hosts free jazz shows by students of the Berklee College of Music in the adjacent outdoor courtyard. *In the Charles Hotel, 1 Bennett St. ☎ 617/395-7757. www.regattabarjazz.com. Tickets $18–$35. T: Harvard. Map p 113.*

★★ **Top of the Hub Jazz Lounge** BACK BAY The ritzy 52nd-floor lounge is a gorgeous

The TV show Cheers ran from 1982 to 1993, and the replica Cheers at Faneuil Hall Marketplace is still a popular walk down memory lane.

setting for romance, especially if you arrive late in the afternoon and watch the sunset. Jazz ensembles perform nightly at 7:30pm. Food options include charcuterie, calamari, burgers, and seafood platters. *Prudential Tower, 800 Boylston St.* ☎ *617/536-1775. www.topofthe hub.net. No cover; no minimum at seats directly at the bar; $24 minimum per person after 8pm at tables. T: Prudential. Map p 114.*

★ **Wally's Cafe** SOUTH END   In the 1940s and 50s, the South End was flush with jazz clubs—the High Hat, Savoy Ballroom, Chicken Lane. Wally's was founded in 1947 by Joseph L. Walcott, said to be the first African American to own a nightclub in New England. Today this teeny venue serves up jazz (but no food) 365 days a year. There's a jam session from 6 to 9pm every evening, often featuring students from neighboring Berklee College of Music, and then jazz, funk, blues, or Latin salsa from 9:30pm to 2am. *427 Massachusetts Ave.* ☎ *617/424-1408. www.wallyscafe.com. No cover. T: Massachusetts Ave. Map p 114.*

LGBTQ Bars & Clubs

★★ **Club Café** SOUTH END The city's top gay nightlife destination has a dance club and a cabaret room that hosts evenings of jazz standards, sing-a-longs, and comedy (Wed–Sun). *209 Columbus Ave.* ☎ *617/536-0966. www.clubcafe.com. No cover Sun–Thurs & until 11pm Fri–Sat. T: Back Bay. Map p 114.*

★ **Jacques** BAY VILLAGE   Here since the 1950s, Boston's only drag club has performances 7 nights a week, with 2 shows on Saturday and participatory events like the Zumba Fitness Dance Party. Lots of evenings it's packed with bachelorette parties. Cash only. *79 Broadway* ☎ *617/426-8902. www.jacques-cabaret.com. Cover $7–$10. T: Arlington. Map p 114.*

Rock & Folk Music Venues

★★ **Blue Hills Bank Pavilion** SEAPORT DISTRICT   Seating 5,000, this outdoor amphitheater is open May through September and brings in big-name, old-school acts such as Jackson Browne, Jethro Tull, and Foreigner. *290 Northern Blvd.* ☎ *617/728-1600. www.bostonpavilion.net. Tickets $65 & way up. T: Northern Ave @ Harbor St. Map p 113.*

★★ **City Winery Boston** HAYMARKET   New in 2017, City Winery lets guests sit, eat, and drink during most shows. Its calendar is eclectic, from Steve Earle to Altan to Sandra Bernhard. *80 Beverly St.* ☎ *617/933-8047. www.citywinery.com/boston. Tickets $15–$60. T: Haymarket. Map p 114.*

★★ **Club Passim** CAMBRIDGE Passim is a Harvard Square landmark for folk music that today features local and national acts 7 nights a week and it offers dinner and a long list of wines and local beers. *47 Palmer St.* ☎ *617/492-7679. www.clubpassim.org. Tickets*

$10–$50 with most shows around $20. T: Harvard. Map p 113.

★ House of Blues FENWAY

Across the street from Fenway Park, this huge club hops year-round with rock, pop, and blues artists. The restaurant serves the chain's familiar Southern menu. *15 Lansdowne St.* ☎ *888/693-2583. www.houseof blues.com/boston. Tickets $23–$55. T: Kenmore. Map p 114.*

★★ The Middle East Restaurant and Nightclub CAMBRIDGE

With three small restaurants and five performance spaces (including a large downstairs room—formerly a bowling alley—a corner bakery, and Sonia, in a room formerly occupied by the equally beloved music club TT the Bears), "The Middle" is an ever-innovative mecca for rock and eclectic alternative music. *472 Massachusetts Ave.* ☎ *617/864-3278. www.mideastclub.com. Most shows $5–$20. T: Central. Map p 113.*

★★★ The Sinclair CAMBRIDGE

This swank gastropub is also the area's first major live music venue. It's comfortable and smartly booked. *52 Church St.* ☎ *617/547-5200. www.sinclaircambridge.com. Tickets $13–$25. T: Harvard. Map p 113.*

Sports Bars

★★ Bleacher Bar FENWAY

Under—under!—the Fenway Park bleachers is this standard-issue ground-floor bar, but with a spectacularly unique feature: a floor-to-ceiling picture window that looks out directly onto centerfield. The bar is accessible from Lansdowne Street, meaning you don't have to be in the stadium to get in. Prime tables enjoy a fielder's-eye view through one-way glass. On evenings when Fenway Park hosts musical events, a seat here gives you a peek at the backstage and the full show for the cost of a burger. *82A Lansdowne St.* ☎ *617/262-2424. www.bleacherbar boston.com. T: Kenmore. Map p 114.*

★ Cask 'n Flagon FENWAY

A local landmark, "The Cask" is busiest when the Red Sox are in town—the team plays across the street at Fenway Park—but lively year-round. Gigantic high-def TV screens at every turn and an outdoor urban patio make this a fun option if you don't want to spring for pricey baseball tickets. *62 Brookline Ave.* ☎ *617/536-4840. www.casknflagon. com. T: Kenmore. Map p 114.*

★★ The Fours NORTH STATION

For hockey and basketball fans, the Fours, across the street from the TD Garden where the Bruins and Celtics play, has been a favorite since 1976. Families will feel comfortable here. *166 Canal St.* ☎ *617/720-4455. www.thefours. com. T: North Station. Map p 114.*

★ Game On! FENWAY

This high-tech "sports cafe" and its dozens of TVs sit in the shadows of left field. Come early for a seat on game days. *82 Lansdowne St.* ☎ *617/351-7001. www.gameonboston.com. T: Kenmore. Map p 114.* ●

Swing Dancing in Boston

Boston has a big swing dance community, with dances in the area 4 to 5 nights a week. **Dance Net** (www.havetodance.com) does yeoman's work keeping a calendar with links to events, many of which feature live swing bands. Argentinean tango dance parties are also listed at the site.

Boston Arts & Entertainment

Agganis Arena 2
AMC Loews Boston Common 19
American Repertory
  Theater (A.R.T.) 1
ArtsEmerson 22
Berklee Performance Center 10
Blue Man Group
  (at Charles Playhouse) 26
Boch Center 28
BosTix discount tickets
  (Copley Square) 11
  (Faneuil Hall) 18
Boston Ballet 21
Boston Center for the Arts 13

Boston Common 16
Boston Landmarks Orchestra 15
Boston Lyric Opera 25
Boston Opera House 21
Boston Pops 9
Boston Symphony Orchestra 9
Brattle Theatre 1
Charles Playhouse 26
Commonwealth
  Shakespeare Company 16
Coolidge Corner Theatre 2
Cutler Majestic Theatre 25
Cyclorama 13
The Donkey Show (at Oberon) 1

Lechmere Ⓣ
28
Spring St.
Hurley St.
Charles St.
2nd St.
1st St.
Land Blvd.
Cambridge Pkwy.
Longfellow Br.

Albany St.
Vassar St.
Amherst St.
Massachusetts Institute
of Technology
(M.I.T.)
Memorial Dr.
3
Memorial Dr.
CAMBRIDGE
Charles River
Charles River
Esplanade
Memorial Dr.
1
Harvard Br.
Storrow Dr.
Clarendon St.
BACK BAY
Exeter St.
Fairfield St.
Commonwealth Ave.
Gloucester St.
Copley Copley
Sq.
Ⓣ
11
12
Storrow Dr.
Bay State Rd.
BOSTON UNIVERSITY
Beacon St.
Marlborough St.
Hereford St.
Newbury St.
St. James Ave.
John
Hancock
Tower
20
Ⓣ Kenmore
Charlesgate
Massachusetts Ave.
2
2
Boston
Public
Library
Back Bay Ⓣ
Dartmouth St.
2
Lansdowne St.
3
Hynes
Convention Center
10
Boylston St.
PRUDENTIAL
CENTER
Clarendon St.
Carleton St.
4 Fenway Park
Van Ness St.
Edgerly Rd.
Belvidere St.
Prudential Ⓣ
Huntington Ave.
St. Botolph St.
W. Newton St.
28
W. Canton St.
W. Brookline St.
Brookline Ave.
Boylston St.
Jersey St.
FENWAY
Muddy R.
Hemenway St.
Westland Ave.
Symphony Rd.
9 Ⓣ Symphony
Mass.
Ⓣ Ave.
Columbus Ave.
Rutland St.
Peterborough St.
Queensberry St.
Park Dr.
Back Bay
Fens
Gainsborough St.
8
7
St. Stephen St.
Tremont St.
West Concord St.
Palace Rd.
The Fenway
Museum of
Fine Arts
St. Forsyth St.
Ⓣ Northeastern
Northampton St.
Massachusetts Ave.
W. Springfield St.
Worcester St.
5
6
9
Museum
NORTHEASTERN
UNIVERSITY
Huntington Ave.
Ruggles St.
Parker St.
Ⓣ Ruggles
Camden St.
Lenox St.
Kendall St.
Hammond St.
Longwood
Ⓣ
Ward St.
McGreevey St.
Melnea Cass Blvd.
ROXBURY

Arts & Entertainment Best Bets

Best **Concert Hall**
★★★ Symphony Hall, *301 Massachusetts Ave. (p 132)*

Best **18th-Century Flashback**
★★ Handel & Haydn Society, *various locations (p 125)*

Best **Opulent Setting**
★★ Isabella Stewart Gardner Museum, *25 Evans Way. (p 132)*

Best **Edgy Theater**
★★ ArtsEmerson, *559 Washington St. (p 129)*

Best **Broadway-Bound Theater**
★★★ American Repertory Theater (A.R.T.), *64 Brattle St., Cambridge (p 129)*

Best **Free Music Performances**
★★ New England Conservatory, *290 Huntington Ave. (p 125)*

Best **Combination of Classical & Pop Music**
★★★ Boston Pops, *301 Massachusetts Ave. (p 125)*

Best **Classic Classical**
★★★ Boston Symphony Orchestra, *301 Massachusetts Ave. (p 125)*

Best **Sports Stadium**
★★★ Fenway Park, *4 Yawkey Way (p 128)*

Best **Christmas Event**
★★★ *The Nutcracker,* Boston Ballet, *Boston Opera House, 539 Washington St. (p 126)*

Best **Venue for Rising Talent**
★★ Berklee Performance Center, *136 Massachusetts Ave. (p 130)*

Best **Family Entertainment (14+)**
★★ *Shear Madness, Charles Playhouse, 74 Warrenton St. (p 130)*

Best **Free Outdoor Theater**
★★ Commonwealth Shakespeare Company, *Boston Common (p 129)*

Best **First-Run Movie Venue**
★★ ShowPlace Icon, *60 Seaport Blvd. (p 127)*

Best **Movie Screen**
★★ Coolidge Corner Theatre, *290 Harvard St., Brookline (p 126)*

Fenway Park, the home of the Boston Red Sox, is open for tours every day of the year. Page 121: Historic Fenway Park.

Arts & Entertainment A to Z

Keith Lockhart leads the Boston Pops.

Classical Music

★ kids **Boston Landmarks Orchestra** HATCH SHELL   The orchestra performs free concerts on Wednesday nights in July and August at the DCR Hatch Shell next to the Charles River. Check the website for other free shows around town, including on the Rose F. Kennedy Greenway. *Performances at the Hatch Shell and in other locations.* ☎ 617/987-2000. www.landmarks orchestra.org.

★★★ kids **Boston Pops** BACK BAY   The playful sibling of the **Boston Symphony Orchestra** (below), the Pops often features celebrity guest stars. In addition to performances at Symphony Hall, the Pops plays the Fourth of July extravaganza at the DCR Hatch Shell along the Charles River, holiday programs in December, and summer shows at Tanglewood in Western Massachusetts. *301 Massachusetts Ave.* ☎ 888/266-1200 or ☎ 617/266-1200 (SymphonyCharge). www.bostonpops.org. *Tickets $22–$125. T: Symphony.*

★★★ kids **Boston Symphony Orchestra** BACK BAY   One of the city's cultural jewels, the BSO is among the finest orchestras in the world. The most celebrated programs are classical music, often with a renowned guest artist or conductor. The season runs September through May and performances take place in the ornate, airy Symphony Hall. *301 Massachusetts Ave.* ☎ 888/266-1200 (SymphonyCharge). www.bso.org. *Tickets $30–$145; limited availability of $20 tickets for people under 40 and $10 rush tickets. T: Symphony.*

★★ **Emmanuel Music** BACK BAY   The Ensemble-in-Residence at Emmanuel Church, on Newbury Street in the Back Bay, performs afternoon and evening concerts, some at 10pm. The group also presents Bach cantatas during the 10am Sunday services and a free noontime series on Thursdays (see box p 126). *15 Newbury St.* ☎ 617/536-3356. www.emmanuelmusic.org. *Tickets $10–$55, with Christmas concerts $10–$150. T: Arlington.*

★★ **Handel & Haydn Society** BACK BAY   "Historically informed" concerts with Baroque period instruments are presented in dynamic, creative performances. Concerts take place either at Symphony Hall, New England Conservatory's Jordan Hall down the block, or Sanders Theatre in Harvard Square. *Box office: 9 Harcourt St.* ☎ 617/262-1815. www.handel andhaydn.org.

★★ kids **New England Conservatory** BACK BAY   Conservatory students and faculty perform 1,000 concerts a year—classical, jazz, chamber music, and contemporary improv—all for free. There are several performance venues on the campus, including the esteemed Jordan Hall. *290 Huntington Ave.* ☎ 617/585-1260. www.necmusic.edu/ concerts-community. T: Symphony.

Lunchtime Classical at Churches

Most churches offer uplifting liturgical music at Sunday services, but many host classical concerts during the work week as well. On **Tuesdays, King's Chapel** presents a 40-minute recital at 12:15pm, with performances that range from Elizabethan song to Baltic folk music to classical guitar (58 Tremont St., ☎ 617/227-2155; www.kings-chapel.org; $5 donation requested). On **Thursdays, Emmanuel Music** (p 125) puts on free noontime concerts (reserve a spot by phone or online) in the Lindsay Chapel at Emmanuel Church (15 Newbury St., ☎ 617/536-3356; www.emmanuelmusic.org). The **Fridays at Trinity Organ Recital Series** presents 30-minute organ concerts at 12:15pm at Trinity Church, the architectural treasure at the heart of Copley Square (206 Clarendon St., ☎ 617/536-0944; www.trinitychurchboston.org; $10 donation requested).

Dance

★★★ kids Boston Ballet THEATER DISTRICT   One of the top dance companies in the country, the troupe is best known for its annual wintertime performances of *The Nutcracker*, but it presents a full season of classical works from November through June. *Performances at the Boston Opera House* (p 131). ☎ 617/695-6955 (box office). www.bostonballet.org. Tickets $35–$154. T: Park Street.

Film

★ kids AMC Loews Boston Common 19 THEATER DISTRICT The only first-run theater downtown has stadium seating and big crowds on weekend nights. (It also has some competition from the new **ShowPlace Icon,** below.) Tickets can be purchased online in advance. *175 Tremont St.* ☎ 617/423-5801. www.amctheatres.com. Tickets $11–$14. T: Boylston.

★★ kids Brattle Theatre CAMBRIDGE   An enduring repertory house (founded in 1953), the Brattle screens classics like *Casablanca,* plus plenty of indie and foreign films. It also hosts music and book author events. *40 Brattle St.* ☎ 617/876-6837. www.brattlefilm.org. Tickets $8–$11. T: Harvard.

★★ kids Coolidge Corner Theatre BROOKLINE   The great independent art house of the area, the Coolidge has a gorgeous main room (Moviehouse 1) and three smaller theaters. Check here first for independent and international films. There are also midnight

Boston Symphony Orchestra.

Boston Ballet is one of the country's finest dance companies.

★★ ShowPlace Icon SEAPORT DISTRICT   The 2018 landing of this swanky new movie theater in the Seaport District was another step in the cultural development of this neighborhood, giving office workers of the area as well as tourists another reason to stick around in the evenings. It has 10 auditoriums, a lounge menu, and a full bar. *60 Seaport Blvd.* ☎ *857/444-6677. www.bostonseaport.xyz/venue/ showplace-icon-theatre. Tickets $17–$22. T: Courthouse.*

screenings and twice monthly baby-friendly screenings in the main theater. *290 Harvard St.* ☎ *617/734-2500. www.coolidge. org. Tickets $11–$13. T: Coolidge Corner.*

★★ Kendall Square Cinema CAMBRIDGE   The Kendall offers independent and foreign-language films (and has excellent concessions). *1 Kendall Sq.* ☎ *617/621-1202). www.landmarktheatres.com. Tickets $11–$13. T: Red Line to Kendall/MIT, 10-min. walk.*

Opera

★★ kids Boston Lyric Opera THEATER DISTRICT   With four productions a year—in the 2017–2018 season they included "Tosca" and "The Threepenny Opera"—the BLO works hard to make opera accessible, offering two-show subscriptions and a few $25 tickets at each performance, and even reassuring guests that it's OK to wear jeans. Productions are held at the **Cutler Majestic Theatre** (p 131), **Huntington Theatre** (p 130), and **Cyclorama** at the BCA (p 131). ☎ *617/542-6772. www.blo.org. Tickets $32–$262.*

Christmas in Boston

Starting in late November, Boston becomes a wonderland of tiny twinkling lights and decorated Christmas trees, with special holiday programing to match. In addition to the annual performances of *The Nutcracker* by **Boston Ballet** and the **Christmas Revels** extravaganza (both detailed on p 126), performances include the Boston Pops **Holiday Pops** concerts (www.bso.org); **Black Nativity,** the National Center of Afro-American Artists' annual (on track for its 50th anniversary in 2020) presentation of Langston Hughes' song-play (www.blacknativity.org); and **A Christmas Celtic Sojourn** of Celtic, Pagan, and Christian music of the season, hosted by WGBH radio host Brian O'Donovan.

Take Yourself Out to the Ballgame

You may have heard that Boston has a thing for sports. The city is home to wildly successful pro teams in baseball (Red Sox), basketball (Celtics), hockey (Bruins), and football (New England Patriots). It also cheers on a pro soccer team (New England Revolution), a thriving roller derby league, world-class runners and the annual Boston Marathon, and rowers who travel from around the world to the Head of the Charles Regatta each October. Homegrown stars include Olympic gymnast Aly Raisman and 2017 NYC Marathon winner Shalane Flanagan, and the high school girls field hockey team in nearby Watertown had a nine-year best-in-the-nation unbeaten streak until a loss in 2017—its first in 184 games. Tickets to stadium events can be purchased at team websites or at Stubhub, a ticket-trading site owned by eBay and sanctioned by the teams; the Marathon and Regatta are free to watch from the sidelines. The nationally broadcast sports radio show "Only a Game" originates here, at WBUR. And baseball fans will want to check out the Twitter feed of Josh Kantor (@jtkantor), the ballpark organist for the Red Sox—tweet a request to him and he'll try to include it during the game.

Sports & More

★ **kids** **Agganis Arena** BOSTON UNIVERSITY BU's hockey rink is home to the school's men's hockey team (the women's team plays at the 3,806-seat Walter Brown Arena around the corner). Touring artists such as Bob Dylan and family shows like Disney on Ice also do shows here. *925 Commonwealth Ave.* ☎ *617/358-7000 or* ☎ *800/745-3000 (Ticketmaster). www.agganis arena.com. Ticket prices vary. T: St. Paul St.*

★★★ **kids** **Fenway Park** FENWAY The city's beloved **Red Sox** play at the landmark ballpark from April to October. Concerts are held here when the team is away, with big names such as Jay Z & Justin Timberlake, Dead & Company, and Journey. See p 18, ⑫. *4 Jersey St. (formerly Yawkey Way)* ☎ *877/RED-SOX-9. www.redsox.com. Tickets $10–$197. T: Kenmore.*

★ **kids** **Gillette Stadium** FOXBOROUGH, MA Boston's baseball, basketball, and hockey teams play right downtown, but to see the storied **New England Patriots** football team you have to travel 28 miles southwest to the suburban town of Foxborough, where the team plays at the 65,878 capacity Gillette Stadium. In addition to Pats games, Gillette also hosts games by the **New England Revolution** soccer team, a variety of other sporting events, and big-name musical acts such as Taylor Swift and Kenny Chesney. *One Patriot Place, Foxborough.* ☎ *508/543-8200. www.gillettestadium.com. Tickets vary.*

★ **kids** **Lucky Strike Social Boston** FENWAY This 3-story complex across the street from Fenway Park was undergoing changes in 2018. It encompasses 16 bowling lanes, a floor of video and arcade games, some billiard tables, and

Cheeky Monkey Brewing Co. and restaurant. It's a rebranded and redesigned Jillian's—the giant pool hall complex that ruled here for 30 years and whose branding is not quite phased out. Children are welcome during the day. *145 Ipswich St.* ☎ *617/437-0300. www.jillians boston.com. T: Kenmore, 10-min. walk.*

★ kids **TD Garden** NORTH STA-TION The city's premier arena is home to the **Celtics** (National Basketball Association) and **Bruins** (National Hockey League), both of which draw huge crowds of diehard fans. "The Garden" also brings in ice shows and touring rock and pop artists such as Bon Jovi and Maroon 5. *100 Legends Way* ☎ *617/624-1331. www.tdgarden.com. Ticket prices vary. T: North Station.*

Theater Companies & Shows (also see Venues)
★★ **ArtsEmerson** THEATER DIS-TRICT ArtsEmerson burst onto the scene and immediately established itself as one of the city's most exciting presenting and producing organizations. Sponsored by Emerson College, it says this of its mission: "Founded in 2010, the year the US Census confirmed there was no single cultural majority in Boston, we committed to building a cultural institution that reflects the diversity of our city." Theater, dance, and film are central, with

events that include "Citizen Read," a public dialogue on race and identity in America. Its **Emerson Para-mount Center** has three theaters, and it also presents work at Emerson's **Cutler Majestic Theatre** (p 131). *559 Washington St.* ☎ *617/824-8400. www.artsemerson.org and www.emersonparamount.org. Ticket prices vary. T: Boylston.*

★★★ **American Repertory Theater (A.R.T.)** CAMBRIDGE Founded in 1980, the nationally renowned A.R.T. (say each letter) is associated with Harvard. Internationally celebrated artistic director Diane Paulus brought pizazz to the programming, and many productions move on to Broadway. Performances are at two venues at either side of Harvard Square: the main **Loeb Drama Center** to the north and club **Oberon** to the south, at 0 Arrow St. *64 Brattle St.* ☎ *617/547-8300. www.amrep.org. Tickets $25 and up. T: Harvard.*

★★ kids **Blue Man Group** THE-ATER DISTRICT The long-running percussive phenom features a trio of cobalt-colored performers backed by a rock band. They enlist audience members, so be ready if you're sitting in the first few rows. *Charles Playhouse, 74 Warrenton St.* ☎ *800/BLUEMAN. www.blueman. com. Tickets $66-$170. T: Boylston.*

★★ kids **Commonwealth Shakespeare Company** BOS-TON COMMON A highlight of

Boston's Best Arts Media

For up-to-date information on arts events, check the websites for **WBUR Artery** (www.wbur.org/artery), *Boston* magazine (www. bostonmagazine.com), and *Scout Cambridge* (www.scout cambridge.com). Also look for the free magazines *Improper Bostonian* and *DigBoston* in sidewalk boxes.

summer is the company's "Shake-speare on the Common," a free production outdoors on the Boston Common at the Parkman Band-stand. Performances take place Tuesday through Sunday at 8pm, usually mid-July through early August. Bring a blanket to sit on the lawn or rent a lawn chair for $5. *Boston Common.* ☎ *617/426-0863. www.commshakes.org. Free admission. T: Park Street.*

★★ The Donkey Show CAM-

BRIDGE Get your Bacchanalian on at this gyrating, disco version of Shakespeare's *A Midsummer Night's Dream.* The performance unfolds every Saturday at 10:30pm in club Oberon, among patrons who drink and dance alongside the slinky per-formers. The club stays open for dancing after the show. *2 Arrow St.* ☎ *617/547-8300. www.amrep.org. Tickets $25–$45. T: Harvard.*

★★ Huntington Theatre Com-

pany FENWAY The well-regarded Huntington presents both contem-porary works and revivals. Some productions take place at the Bos-ton Center for the Arts (p 131). *264 Huntington Ave.* ☎ *617/266-0800. www.huntingtontheatre.org. Ticket prices vary. T: Symphony.*

★★ kids Shear Madness THE-

ATER DISTRICT Since 1980, audi-ences have been helping solve a murder in this madcap show set in a hair salon. It's great fun and never the same twice. *Charles Playhouse Stage II, 74 Warrenton St.* ☎ *617/ 426-5225. www.shearmadness.com. Tickets $56. T: Boylston.*

Venues (Theater, Music, Dance & More)

★★ Berklee Performance Cen-

ter BACK BAY Students and staff members from Berklee's noted jazz programs perform here, as do tour-ing artists and speakers. *136 Massa-chusetts Ave.* ☎ *617/747-2261. www.berklee.edu/BPC. Tickets $8 and up. T: Hynes Convention Center.*

★★ kids Boch Center THEATER

DISTRICT Two historic venues make up the nonprofit Boch Center. The grand **Wang Theatre,** a former movie house that was restored in the 1980s and now seats 3,500. Across the street, the **Shubert The-atre** is a medium-size venue that's perfect for musicals, opera, and dance productions. *Wang Theatre & box office for both: 270 Tremont St.* ☎ *800/982-2787. www.bochcenter.*

American Repertory Theater (A.R.T.) in Cambridge presents dramas as well as musicals, such as Pippin.

Getting a Deal on Tickets

ArtsBoston (calendar.artsboston.org; ☎ 617/262-8632 x229) is an excellent resource for cultural listings and ticket deals. It runs the BosTix discount-ticket service that includes programming from over 100 area performing-arts organizations. Tickets are available online, by phone, or at **BosTix booths** at Faneuil Hall Marketplace (T: Government Center) and in Copley Square, at the corner of Boylston Street and Dartmouth Street (T: Copley). Tickets are 20 to 80% off the original ticket price, with most at 50% off. There is a service fee of up to $8.50 per ticket, even for in-person purchases. The Faneuil Hall booth is open Thursday through Sunday from 10am to 4pm. The Copley Square booth is open Tuesday through Friday 11am to 5pm, Saturday and Sunday from 10am to 4pm.

org. Shubert: 265 Tremont St. ☎ 866/348-9738. Tickets $35 and up. T: Boylston.

★★ Boston Center for the Arts

SOUTH END   The BCA complex is home to artists' studios and rehearsal spaces, the Mills art gallery, a couple of good bars, and six theaters, including the **Wimberly Theatre** in the Calderwood Pavilion, the **BCA Plaza Black Box Theatre,** and the **Cyclorama**. 539 Tremont St. ☎ 617/426-5000. www. bcaonline.org. Tickets $10–$38; some shows free. T: Back Bay.

★★ kids Boston Opera House

THEATER DISTRICT   Although it's called an opera house, touring Broadway musicals play here, and the **Boston Ballet** and The Nutcracker hold court from Thanksgiving through New Year. The theater was built as an ornate vaudeville house in the 1920s and finished a gorgeous $54-million restoration in 2004. 539 Washington St. ☎ 617/259-3400. Tickets from Ticketmaster ☎ 800/982-2787. www.bostonopera house.com. Ticket prices vary. T: Park Street.

★★ Cutler Majestic Theatre

THEATER DISTRICT   The exquisite 1903 Beaux Arts facility books international theater, dance, and opera, as well as one-time events like The Moth StorySLAM. 219 Tremont St. ☎ 617/824-8000. www.cutler majestic.org. Ticket prices vary. T: Boylston.

★★ Emerson Colonial Theatre

THEATER DISTRICT   Closed for a few years while owner Emerson College deliberated its fate, the historic building reopened in 2018 with a 40-year partnership with London's Ambassador Theatre Group, which will develop the programming. The theater was built in 1900 and premiered seminal musicals

Commonwealth Shakespeare Company's The Last Will.

The Wang Theatre in the Boch Center opened in 1925 and seats 3,500.

such as *Anything Goes, Oklahoma!, La Cage aux Folles,* and, in 1935, *Porgy and Bess.* 106 Boylston St. ☎ 888/616-0272. www.emerson colonialtheatre.com. Ticket prices vary. T: Boylston.

★★ kids **Hatch Shell** BACK BAY The riverside amphitheater, best known as the home of the Boston Pops' Fourth of July concert, schedules other events on many summer nights. Family-friendly Free Friday Flicks begin at sunset. *Charles River Esplanade.* ☎ 617/727-4708. www. mass.gov/locations/charles-river-reservation. Free admission. T: Charles/MGH.

★★ **Isabella Stewart Gardner Museum** FENWAY The magnificent museum (p 23, ③) has an innovative programming calendar

featuring not just chamber music but also jazz and modern special events such as The Red Party, which "brings together fashion, music, and technology." In addition to performances within the galleries of the museum itself, events are also held in the Calderwood Hall "sonic cube" that holds 300 people. Mrs. Gardner would have approved. *25 Evans Way.* ☎ 617/566-1401. www. isgm.org. Tickets vary and include museum admission. T: Museum of Fine Arts.

★★ kids **Museum of Fine Arts** FENWAY The museum (p 22, ①) provides an appealing backdrop for indoor and outdoor performances by a variety of global artists. *465 Huntington Ave.* ☎ 800/440-6975. www.mfa.org/programs/music. Tickets $16–$30; some events free with museum admission. T: Museum of Fine Arts.

★ **Orpheum Theatre** DOWNTOWN CROSSING Centrally located just around the corner from the Boston Common and Park Street T station, the 1852 building is rickety and cramped but still gets bookings such as Robert Plant, k. d. lang, and Peppa Pig. *1 Hamilton Place* ☎ 617/482-0106 or ☎ 800/745-3000 (Ticketmaster). www.cross roadspresents.com. Ticket prices vary. T: Park St.

★★★ **Symphony Hall** FENWAY Primarily host to the resident BSO and Boston Pops, Symphony Hall books other musical artists and speakers into its acoustically perfect hall. *301 Massachusetts Ave.* ☎ 888/266-1200 (SymphonyCharge). www.bso.org. Ticket prices vary. T: Symphony. ●

Lodging Best Bets

Best **Boston Hotel**
★★★ Boston Harbor Hotel $$$ *Rowes Wharf (p 135)*

Best **Cambridge Hotel**
★★★ The Charles Hotel $$$ *1 Bennett St. (p 138)*

Best **Luxury Hotel**
★★★ Four Seasons Hotel $$$$ *200 Boylston St. (p 140)*

Best **Romantic Hotel**
★★★ Eliot Hotel $$$ *370 Commonwealth Ave. (p 139)*

Best **Hot New Hotel**
★★ The Godfrey $$$ *505 Washington St. (p 140)*

Best **Historic Hotel**
★★ Fairmont Copley Plaza Hotel $$$ *138 St. James Ave. (p 139)*

Best **Hotel That Was Once a Jail**
★★ The Liberty $$$ *215 Charles St. (p 142)*

Best **Family Hotels**
★★ Boston Marriott Long Wharf $$$ *296 State St. (p 135)*; ★★ Colonnade Hotel Boston $$ *120 Huntington Ave. (p 139)*; ★★ Residence Inn by Marriott Boston Downtown/ Seaport $$ *370 Congress St. (p 142)*; ★★ Royal Sonesta Hotel $$$ *40 Edwin H. Land Blvd. (p 142)*

Best **Rock 'n' Roll Hotel**
★★ Verb $$$ *1271 Boylston St. (p 143)*

Best **City Views**
★★★ The Westin Copley Place Boston $$$ *10 Huntington Ave. (p 144)*

Best **Access to the Charles River**
★★ Kimpton Marlowe Hotel $$$ *25 Edwin H. Land Blvd., Cambridge (p 141)*

The Charles Hotel, in Harvard Square, is one of the finest hotels in Cambridge. Previous page: Fairmont Copley Plaza.

Cambridge Lodging

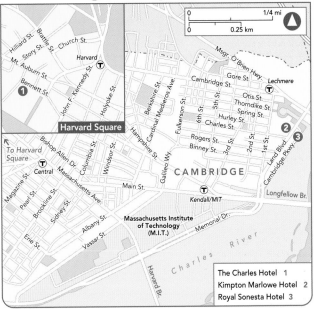

The Charles Hotel	1
Kimpton Marlowe Hotel	2
Royal Sonesta Hotel	3

Lodging A to Z

★★★ Boston Harbor Hotel

WATERFRONT   Majestic and sweeping, with a 60-foot stone archway at its entrance, this hotel has become a signature structure along Boston's gracefully renovated harbor. It boasts gorgeous rooms to match its exterior, with marble bathrooms, expansive views of either the water or the Boston city skyline, and courtly service. Its **Rowes Wharf Sea Grille** has an appealing outdoor terrace in warm weather in an enclave alongside the harbor walk. *70 Rowes Wharf.* ☎ *800/752-7077. www.bhh.com. 230 units. Doubles $315–$1,045. T: Aquarium. Map p 136.*

★★ kids Boston Marriott Long Wharf WATERFRONT   Across the street from **Faneuil Hall Marketplace,** next to the **New England Aquarium** (p 12, ⑩), and directly on the Boston harbor, this hotel is perfectly located for families. A small pool has glassed-in walls and an outside deck to catch some rays. Rooms were renovated in 2018. *296 State St.* ☎ *617/227-0800. www. marriott.com/boslw. 412 units. Doubles $265–$600. T: Aquarium. Map p 136.*

★★ Boston Park Plaza BACK
BAY   If you're looking for a bit of glamour without the price tag of the city's very highest-end options, the updated Park Plaza could be

Boston Lodging

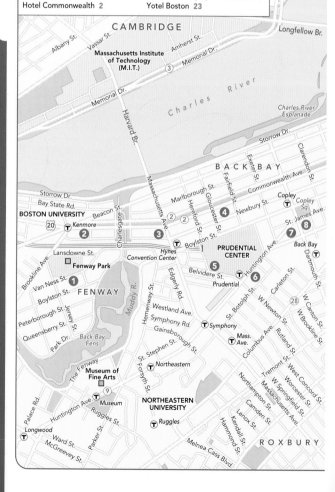

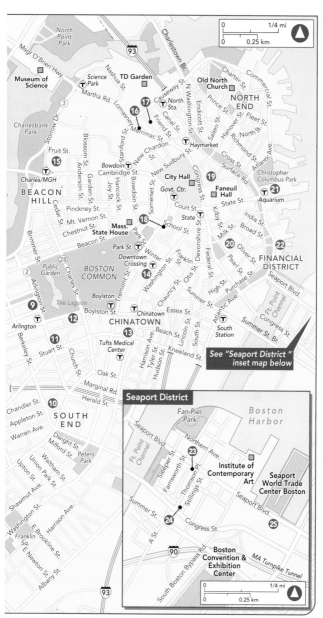

The Boston Harbor Hotel's arch is a defining feature of the Boston waterfront.

just the ticket. A $100-million renovation completed in 2016 has spruced up the 1927 building, from the soaring lobby and grand ballroom to guest rooms, which have all been renovated. Keep in mind that the smallest units, called "Run of the House," are just 150 sq. ft. With a lot of rooms to fill and a hunger to reestablish itself as a go-to option, prices are competitive. *50 Park Plaza.* ☎ *617/426-2000. www.bostonparkplaza.com. 1,060 units. Doubles $179–$350. T: Arlington. Map p 136.*

★ **The Bostonian** FANEUIL HALL MARKETPLACE   Three renovated 19th-century buildings make up this stylish hotel directly across the street from **Faneuil Hall** (p 9) and on the Freedom Trail, putting visitors in the heart of Boston's historic tourist area. Some rooms have balconies, and others have fireplaces. *26 North St.* ☎ *617/523-3600. www. millenniumhotels.com/en/boston. 204 units. Doubles $188–$475. T: Government Center. Map p 136.*

★★ **The Boxer Hotel** NORTH STATION   Like the **Kimpton Onyx Hotel** (p 141) around the block, this boutique hotel, opened in 2013 in a repurposed 1904 building, is in a neighborhood that is in a state of redevelopment. It has a slate grey industrial look that highlights a fashion-forward urban design, with rooms that are small but sleek. The Boxer is the exclusive hotel partner of **City Winery Boston** (p 119), a music and dining space a 5-minute walk from the front door. *107 Merrimac St.* ☎ *617/624-0202. theboxer boston.com. 80 units. Doubles $220–$485. T: Haymarket. Map p 136.*

★★ **The Chandler Inn Hotel** SOUTH END   This 56-unit boutique hotel is located in the residential South End, the city's predominant gay neighborhood. It's a good choice to get a taste of Boston that's just off the tourist track. Rooms are small, with no closets and tight bathroom quarters, but its ground floor **Trophy Room** restaurant and bar often stays busy until 2am. *26 Chandler St.* ☎ *800/842-3450. www.chandlerinn. com. 56 units. Doubles $118–$249. T: Back Bay. Map p 136.*

★★★ kids **The Charles Hotel** CAMBRIDGE   Tucked into the side of Harvard Square next to Harvard University's Kennedy School, Cambridge's finest hotel boasts top-notch accommodations, access to a

Hotel Alternatives

Bed-and-breakfasts boast homey settings, give visitors an opportunity to connect with locals, and are often less expensive than hotels. The **Greater Boston Convention & Visitors Bureau** maintains a small list of B&Bs and inns that it recommends, at www.bostonusa.com/hotels/bed-and-breakfast-inns. **Airbnb** lists over 300 rentals of single rooms and whole apartments in Boston, at www.airbnb.com/s/BostonMA.

high-end health club and spa, and an in-house jazz club (**Regattabar**, p 118). The good-size rooms mix-and-match styles: Unfussy New England Shaker touches contrast with pampering details. *1 Bennett St. Cambridge.* ☎ *800/882-1818. www.charleshotel.com. 294 units. Doubles from $250. T: Harvard. Map p 135.*

★★ kids **Colonnade Hotel Boston** BACK BAY   Contemporary boutique style, old-fashioned service, and large guest rooms draw business travelers, while families come for all that plus an outdoor rooftop pool (May–Sept). The appealing **Brasserie JO** (p 103) is the in-house restaurant. Booking online provides choice benefits

including, 2pm checkout, a restaurant discount, and an upgrade at check-in. *120 Huntington Ave.* ☎ *800/962-3030. www.colonnade hotel.com. 285 units. Doubles $189–$309. T: Prudential. Map p 136.*

★★★ **Eliot Hotel** BACK BAY   A standout, even in a city with lots of exquisite options. Most units in this elegant, boutique hotel are large, romantic suites with antique furnishings. That gives the Eliot a residential feel, with a gracious staff completing the illusion. *370 Commonwealth Ave.* ☎ *800/443-5468. www.eliothotel.com. 95 units. Doubles from $215. T: Hynes Convention Center. Map p 136.*

★★ **Fairmont Copley Plaza Hotel** BACK BAY   Ornate decor

Colonnade Hotel Boston has one of the city's few rooftop pools.

and courtly service make this hotel, built in 1912, a Boston classic. Posh furnishings will make you feel at home—if "home" is a mansion. The Copley Square location, across from the Boston Public Library, puts the elegant hotel in the center of the city and just steps from shopping on Newbury Street and in the malls at Copley Place and the Prudential Center. A rooftop health club has panoramic windows overlooking Back Bay, and its **OAK Long Bar + Kitchen** (p 117) is glamorous. As with other Fairmont properties, pricier Fairmont Gold rooms include a private lounge serving evening hors d'oeuvres and a continental breakfast. *138 St. James Ave.* ☎ *866/540-4417. www.fairmont.com/copley plaza. 383 units. Doubles from $229. T: Copley. Map p 136.*

★★★ kids Four Seasons Hotel BACK BAY Beautiful, expensive, and one of the loveliest hotels in New England, the Four Seasons offers its pampered guests everything they could ever want—for a price. It looks out onto the sublime Boston Public Garden and is close to everything. All rooms were renovated in 2017, heightening the elegance and sophistication of this property. Amenities include an indoor pool with floor to ceiling windows and a private Boston Duck Boat tour. The in-house **Bristol Bar** gets consistently good notice for its atmosphere and food. *200 Boylston St.* ☎ *617/338-4400. www.fourseasons.com/boston. 273 units. Doubles from $605. T: Arlington. Map p 136.*

★★ The Godfrey DOWNTOWN CROSSING Do you hear that buzz? The Godfrey opened in early 2016 and was immediately christened one of the coolest new urban hotels in the country by *Travel + Leisure*. Visitors and other press began heaping similar accolades on the facility, terming it "refined simplicity" and raving about **Ruka** (declared one of the city's "sexiest new restaurants" by *Zagat*), its bar (bartender Will Thompson was named best in the city by *Boston* magazine) and its cafe (run by Boston coffee master George Howell). *505 Washington St.* ☎ *855/649-4500. www.godfreyhotelboston.com. 242 units. Doubles $269 & up. T: Downtown Crossing. Map p 136.*

★ Hostelling International Boston THEATER DISTRICT Well located in the theater district around the corner from the **Wilbur**

Eliot Hotel offers large, romantic suites—and a critically acclaimed in-house Japanese restaurant, Uni.

Fairmont Copley Plaza is the "grande dame" of Boston.

(p 118) and the **Boch Center** (p 130) and a few blocks from the **Boston Common** (p 88), this six-story hostel is popular year-round. Shared dorms and private rooms with their own bathrooms are available. Linens and blankets are provided and the hostel is open 24 hours a day. *19 Stuart St. ☎ 888/464-4872. www.bostonhostel.org. 481 beds. Dorm beds $30–$65, private units $100–$230 w/breakfast. T: Boylston. Map p 136.*

★★ Hotel Commonwealth

FENWAY In 2015, the hotel added 96 rooms in a $50-million expansion that included a new terrace with a view (across the Mass. Pike) of Fenway Park. As the *Boston Globe* raved: "With mod lighting, cool wall art, a sofa that resembled a Chanel jacket, a sleek bathroom, and a lot of houndstooth upholstery. . . this is exactly what a hotel room should look and feel like." It was awarded Best of Boston by *Boston* magazine in 2017. The hotel is convenient to Boston University as well as the baseball park. *500 Commonwealth Ave. ☎ 866/784-4000. www.hotelcommonwealth.com. 245 units. Doubles $179–$529. T: Kenmore. Map p 136.*

★★ kids Kimpton Marlowe Hotel

CAMBRIDGE This posh business hotel near MIT and the Museum of Science also appeals to families, thanks to its good-sized rooms that are elegantly decorated with funky accents. The hotel has an appealing courtyard that faces a small canal inlet off the Charles River, and free kayaks and bikes for borrowing. *25 Edwin H. Land Blvd. ☎ 800/825-7140. www.hotel marlowe.com. 236 units. Doubles $146–$330. T: Lechmere. Map p 135.*

★★ Kimpton Onyx Hotel

NORTH STATION Close to Boston's Italian North End neighborhood and just a block from the TD Garden, the Onyx is an obvious option for visitors who are seeing a concert or sports event at the stadium. The hotel's contemporary boutique decor befits the gentrifying neighborhood. As with many hotels in Boston, pets are welcome here. *155 Portland St. ☎ 866/660-6699. www.onyxhotel.com. 112 units. Doubles $175–$390. T: Haymarket. Map p 136.*

★★ The Langham, Boston

FINANCIAL DISTRICT Busy with business visitors during the week, the Langham does weekend leisure business at discounted prices. The fitness center has a small lap pool surrounded by atrium windows. An Afternoon Tea includes sweet and savory nibbles and house tea served on Wedgwood china. Updates are scheduled for 2018. *250 Franklin St.* ☎ *617/423-2844. www.boston.langhamhotels.com. 317 units. Doubles $239–$594. T: State. Map p 136.*

★★ The Liberty BEACON HILL

For some people, this will be a kick: a hotel stay in a former Boston lockup. From 1851 to 1990, the soberly dramatic Charles Street Jail served as the detention facility for Suffolk County. In a first-rate example of historic preservation and urban reuse, renovations turned the facility into an unlikely luxury hotel while keeping distinctly jail-like features: an inner atrium with soaring ceilings and walkways lining the perimeter of upper floors, heavy wrought iron doors, and a former "drunk tank" with barred windows that now houses the hotel bar, **Alibi.** A hidden courtyard once served as the exercise yard for prisoners. The location is a good one, at the base of the lovely Charles Street shopping destination and residential Beacon Hill. The on-site restaurant **Scampo** (Italian for "escape") is helmed by esteemed chef-owner Lydia Shire. *215 Charles St.* ☎ *617/224-4000. www.liberty hotel.com. 298 units. Doubles $149–$515. T: Charles/MGH. Map p 136.*

★ Newbury Guest House

BACK BAY   Housed in a trio of converted 1880s town houses, this sophisticated inn offers comfortable accommodations and New England charm. It's located on fashionable Newbury Street, one of the city's favorite boutique and walking thoroughfares. Full breakfast is included. *261 Newbury St.* ☎ *800/437-7668. www.newburyguesthouse. com. 32 units. Doubles $129–$429 w/*

breakfast. *T: Hynes Convention Center. Map p 136.*

★ kids Omni Parker House

DOWNTOWN CROSSING   In business since 1855 ("America's longest continuously operating hotel"), the Parker House offers a range of rooms, with most on the extremely compact end of the scale. The public spaces have a 19th-century old-world grandeur, and the hotel is right on the Freedom Trail. But its real claim to fame is being the acknowledged inventor of both the Boston cream pie and buttery Parker House dinner rolls. Both are available here and generate their own tourist traffic. *60 School St.* ☎ *888/444-6664. www. omniparkerhouse.com. 551 units. Doubles $99–$530. T: Government Center. Map p 136.*

★★ kids Residence Inn by Marriott Boston Downtown / Seaport SEAPORT DISTRICT

Name notwithstanding, this hotel is squarely in the Seaport District (not downtown), in a central location close to excellent restaurants, the Boston Children's Museum, and the convention center. In a former life, the historical building was a 1901 warehouse, and rooms boast 12-foot ceilings and exposed beams and brick. All rooms are studios or one-bedroom suites, all with fully equipped kitchens. *370 Congress St.* ☎ *617/478-0840. www.marriott.com/bosfp. 120 units. Doubles $214–$434 w/breakfast. T: Courthouse. Map p 136.*

★★ kids Royal Sonesta Hotel

CAMBRIDGE   Like **the Kimpton Marlowe Hotel** (p 141) across the street, this luxurious hotel offers easy access to MIT, the Museum of Science, and Boston itself. Spacious rooms provide river and city views, and there's an atrium-style lap pool

The stately Omni Parker House, in business since 1855.

with natural light from sliding glass walls and a sun deck in summer. *40 Edwin H. Land Blvd.* ☎ *617/806-4200. www.sonesta.com/boston. 400 units. Doubles $159–$529. T: Lechmere. Map p 135.*

★★ kids **Seaport Hotel** SEAPORT DISTRICT A business-traveler favorite—it's across the street from the World Trade Center Boston and boasts a sleek fitness center. The expansive hotel also attracts families for its kid-savvy staff, heated indoor pool, and proximity to the **Boston Children's Museum** (p 29). *1 Seaport Lane.* ☎ *877/732-7678. www.seaport boston.com. 428 units. Doubles $152–$413. T: World Trade Center. Map p 136.*

★★ kids **Sheraton Boston Hotel** BACK BAY Huge and well-appointed (large indoor/outdoor pool, fitness center, spa and salon), this Sheraton has a central location next to the Hynes Convention Center, the Prudential Center shopping mall, and the Copley Place mall. *39 Dalton St.* ☎ *617/236-2000. www.sheratonbostonhotel. com. 1,220 units. Doubles $150–$450. T: Prudential. Map p 136.*

★★ **Taj Boston** BACK BAY With a peerless location facing the idyllic Boston Public Garden, this property was a Ritz-Carlton before the Indian luxury chain took it over. The first-floor bar has floor-to-ceiling windows that face the Garden, while the elegant French Room serves afternoon tea and the rooftop dining room hosts a Sunday brunch from March to November. The hotel was purchased by a group of local real estate firms in 2016, so change may be in its future. *15 Arlington St.* ☎ *617/536-5700. www.tajhotels.com/boston. 273 units. Doubles from $195. T: Arlington. Map p 136.*

★★ **Verb** FENWAY With Verb, Boston finally gets the rock 'n' roll hotel it deserves. Unveiled in 2014 in a renovated 1959 motel, Verb sits in the shadow of Fenway Park and is rich in the neighborhood's rock history—and managed with care by the former GM of the Four Seasons Hotel Boston. Artwork includes framed covers of the old pop culture magazine *Boston Phoenix* and photos from the beloved Kenmore Square punk venue The Rat. Rooms surround an outdoor pool and have their own turntables—there are LPs

Artful rooms at the Royal Sonesta Hotel in Cambridge look out onto the Charles River and Boston skyline.

in the lobby to borrow. *1271 Boylston St.* ☎ *617/566-4500. www. theverbhotel.com. 93 units. Doubles $169–$459. T: Kenmore. Map p 136.*

★★★ kids **The Westin Copley Place Boston** BACK BAY Guest rooms—all of which were renovated in 2018—are located on floors 8 through 36, providing spectacular views of the city. River views are the prettiest, and priciest. There's an in-house spa (with optional in-room treatments) and a 24-hr. fitness center. *10 Huntington Ave.* ☎ *617/262-9600. www.westin.com/copleyplace. 803 units. Doubles $151–$489. T: Copley. Map p 136.*

★ **Yotel Boston** SEAPORT DIS-TRICT New in 2017 and stylish in a bleeding-edge kind of way, this Boston outpost of a small UK-based chain features teeny rooms that it calls "cabins" (inspired, it says, "by the luxury of first-class travel"). They're cleverly designed, but make sure to look at photos before booking to know what you're getting into. There's a lobby-level bar and a 12th-floor rooftop lounge that is popular on DJ nights. A sister restaurant, **Yo! Sushi,** is down the block at 79 Seaport Blvd. (yosushiusa.com; ☎ 857/400-0797). *65 Seaport Blvd.* ☎ *617/377-4747. www.yotel.com/ boston. 326 units. Doubles $115–$400. T: Courthouse. Map p 136.* ●

Concord

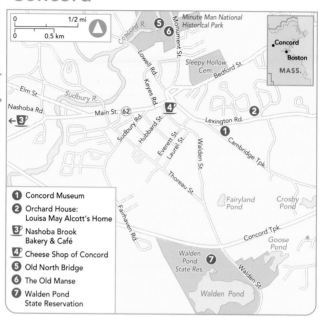

0 ————— 1/2 mi
0 ——— 0.5 km

Minute Man National Historical Park

Sleepy Hollow Cem.

Concord R.

Lowell Rd.

Monument St.

Bedford St.

Elm St.

Sudbury R.

Nashoba Rd.

Main St. 62

Keyes Rd.

Sudbury Rd.

Hubbard St.

Everett St.

Laurel St.

Walden St.

Lexington Rd.

Cambridge Tpk.

Thoreau St.

Fairhaven Rd.

Fairyland Pond

Crosby Pond

Concord Tpk.

Goose Pond

Walden Pond State Res.

Walden St.

Walden Pond

Concord
Boston
MASS.

1 Concord Museum
2 Orchard House: Louisa May Alcott's Home
3 Nashoba Brook Bakery & Café
4 Cheese Shop of Concord
5 Old North Bridge
6 The Old Manse
7 Walden Pond State Reservation

Over the course of three-plus centuries, Concord (pronounced "conquered") has grown from a country village to a prosperous pastoral suburb of about 18,000. The first official battle of the Revolutionary War took place here at the North Bridge on April 19, 1775. By the mid-19th century, an impressive constellation of literary stars—Louisa May Alcott, Ralph Waldo Emerson, Henry Wadsworth Longfellow, and Henry David Thoreau—called the town home. Present-day Concord preserves and honors that rich history.
START: **Drive on Route 2 west from Cambridge. Take exit 50 / MA 2A and stay straight to remain on the Cambridge Turnpike into historic Concord. If it's not rush hour, the trip from Boston takes 30 to 40 minutes.**

1 ★★ kids Concord Museum.
Informative exhibits tell the story of Concord, incorporating artifacts, murals, films, and maps. Originally a Native American settlement, whose tribes lived along the languid Concord River and shared the Algonquian dialect, Concord later became a U.S. Revolutionary War battleground. Still later, it was a literary and intellectual center with a thriving clock-making industry. Many museum displays focus on the big names: You'll see one of the lanterns Longfellow immortalized in "Paul Revere's Ride" ("one if

Previous page: The Mayflower II, *Plymouth's full-scale replica of the* Mayflower.

Walden Pond is a popular spot for swimming and has a reconstructed cabin of author Henry David Thoreau on site.

6 ★ The Old Manse. Next to the Old North Bridge **5**, the Old Manse figures in Concord's rich literary history. Rev. William Emerson built this home in 1770 and watched the terrifying Battle of Concord from its windows. His grandson Ralph Waldo Emerson later worked on the essay "Nature" in the study. Newlywed Nathaniel Hawthorne (*The Scarlet Letter, The House of the Seven Gables*) moved here in 1842. Although he looks forbidding in most of his portraits, on the guided tour of the Old Manse (the only way to see the interior), you'll hear about a lighthearted side: He and Sophia Peabody, who married him, scratched poems to each other on two windows with her diamond ring. ⏱ *1 hr. 269 Monument St. (at North Bridge).* ☎ *978/369-3909. www.oldmanse. org. Guided tour $10 adults, $9 seniors & students, $5 kids 6–12, free for kids 5 & under, $25 families. House: Mid-Apr to Oct Tue–Sun noon–5pm; Nov to mid-Apr Sat–Sun noon–4pm; other times by appointment. Grounds: Year-round daily dawn–dusk.*

7 ★★★ kids Walden Pond State Reservation One of the most famous places in New England is also an attractive, surprisingly unspoiled state park property that allows swimming, fishing, hiking, and picnicking. Walden Pond was home to author Henry David Thoreau for a few years in the mid-1840s—he wrote about his time there and his reflections on life in *Walden*, perhaps the most famous book about living simply—and that legacy helped establish the site as a National Historic Landmark. The wooded park has 462 acres of protected open space. On the shore, there are restrooms at one end of the pond, as well as lifeguards, a sandy beach, and condoned off swimming areas in summer. Hearty swimmers slowly traverse the 1.7-mile circumference, which is 102-foot deep in spots and was created by a melted glacier. A stunning Visitor Center opened in 2016 and is located in the parking lot. Keep in mind that the pond gets half a million visitors a year and on busy days, when it reaches capacity, its parking lot closes for several hours at a time. Check the lot's status on Twitter @waldenpondstate or by calling if you plan to arrive after 9am on a hot day. ⏱ *1–3 hr. 915 Walden St. (Rte. 126), off Route 2.* ☎ *978/369-3254. www. mass.gov/dcr. Parking $8 Mass. residents, $15 non-residents. Free admission to the pond itself. No pets or bikes. Daily 5am–sunset during peak season; check for seasonal hours.*

Salem

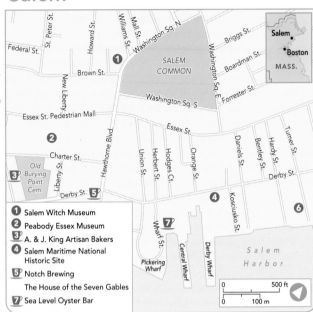

1 Salem Witch Museum
2 Peabody Essex Museum
3 A. & J. King Artisan Bakers
4 Salem Maritime National Historic Site
5 Notch Brewing
   The House of the Seven Gables
7 Sea Level Oyster Bar

If you know Salem only because of its association with witches, you're in for a delightful surprise. Salem has been haunted by the appalling witch trials since 1692, but it has far more history to offer. It was a center of merchant shipping at the height of the post–Revolutionary War China trade, and today Salem celebrates its maritime roots at the same time that it preserves and honors the memory of women and men executed after being accused of witchcraft. START: From downtown Boston, take I-93 north to I-95 north and then Route 128 north. Exit at Route 114 east, and continue to downtown Salem. From Boston, the trip takes about 45 minutes if it isn't rush hour. Plan extra time for travel in October, when Halloween season is in swing.

1 ★ Kids Salem Witch Museum
There are a slew of witch-trial-related sights and walking tours to choose from in Salem and no single option hits every note. Many are seasonal and play up horror over history. This year-round museum provides an informative overview of the 1692

hysteria with a slightly dated presentation: A series of dioramas are populated with life-size human figures that light up in sequence as recorded narration, taken from historic documents, describes the pertinent events. The story is horrifying and grim—most of those accused of "witchcraft" were executed by

The Salem Witch Museum building used to be a church.

hanging, and one was pressed to death by stones piled on a board on his chest—but the anti-prejudice message is both clear and timeless. ⏱ *1 hr. 19½ Washington Sq., at Rte. 1A.* ☎ *978/744-1692. www.salem witchmuseum.com. Admission $12 adults, $10.50 seniors, $9 kids 6–14, free for kids 5 & under. Daily July–Aug 10am–7pm; Sept–June 10am–5pm; check ahead for extended Oct hours.*

❷ ★★★ Peabody Essex Museum

One of New England's premiere art museums, the Peabody Essex originated as a maritime museum (The Peabody) and the county's natural and historical society (the Essex Institute). The two merged in 1992 and have since developed a national reputation for extensive collections of Asian art and photography, American art and architecture, and maritime art. Its curatorial philosophy emphasizes placing objects in context, demonstrating the interplay of influences across time and cultures. The best-known example in the museum's collections is an 18th-century Qing Dynasty house. **Yin Yu Tang,** as the house is known, was shipped to Salem from rural China and is the only example of Chinese domestic architecture

outside that country. Take the audio guide to enjoy an intriguing look at 2 centuries of life in China while exploring the house. Also allow time to check out some of the museum's exceptional traveling shows and lower-profile objects, including regionally made furniture and one of the world's largest shoe collections. ⏱ *3 hr. Build your visit around a timed ticket to Yin Yu Tang. East India Sq., 161 Essex St.* ☎ *866/745-1876 or* ☎ *978/745-9500. www. pem.org. Admission $20 adults, $18*

Yin Yu Tang, a 200-year-old Chinese house, was brought to the U.S. and installed at the Peabody Essex Museum.

The "sky well" of the 16-bedroom Yin Yu Tang house at the Peabody Essex Museum.

seniors, $12 students, free for kids 16 & under. Yin Yu Tang additional $6 fee. Tues–Sun & Mon holidays 10am–5pm.

Not far from the Peabody Essex Museum, ❸ **A. & J. King Artisan Bakers** is a cozy cafe that serves outstanding baked goods and sandwiches on delectable house-made bread. Consider grabbing something—anything!—to go. *48 Central St. ☎ 978/744-4881. www. ajkingbakery.com. $.*

❹ ★ kids **Salem Maritime National Historic Site** Docked in the National Park Service's water-front center is a uniquely memorable exhibit: a full-size (171-ft.) replica of a 1797 East Indiaman merchant vessel. The *Friendship* is open to visitors by guided tour and you can also study it from the shore if you don't want to climb aboard. Note that the ship has been under renovation and is expected to return to Derby Wharf in 2018. Tours also visit other related buildings that touch on Salem's trade and literary history—author Nathaniel Hawthorne, for instance, worked in the Custom House. If this location is closed, visit the Park

Service's regional center at 2 New Liberty St., a 5-minute walk away. ⏱ *1 hr. 193 Derby St. ☎ 978/740-1650. www.nps.gov/sama. Free admission & tours. Summer daily 9am–5pm; winter weekdays 1–5pm, weekends 9am–5pm.*

Kick back with a house brew and a German pretzel while trying your hand at Skee-Ball at ❺ **Notch Brewing** or just hanging out in the Tap Room or year-round biergarten. Kids and dogs are welcome with chaperones. *283R Derby St. ☎ 978/238-9060. www.notchbrewing.com. $–$$.*

❻ ★★ kids **The House of the Seven Gables** Nathaniel Hawthorne wrote the 1851 novel that inspired the name of this attraction (and if you haven't read the book since high school or haven't read it at all, keep in mind that it's scary). Visits to the rambling 1668 house, which celebrates 350 years in 2018, are by guided tour. Tours include details about which elements in the home show up in the book—there's a secret staircase!—and stories of what life in the 1700s was like. The modest home where Hawthorne was born has been moved to the

Salem: Practical Matters

Driving to Salem offers the most flexibility, but the city is also accessible by public transit and easy to negotiate on foot. The **MBTA** (☎ 800/392-6100 or ☎ 617/222-3200; www.mbta.com) operates commuter trains from Boston's North Station and buses from Haymarket. From late May through October, the **Salem Ferry** (☎ 877/733-9425 or ☎ 617/227-4321; www.salemferry.com) leaves from Long Wharf in Boston (next to the New England Aquarium) and is an excellent alternative. Always be sure you know the schedule for your return trip. Tourist information is widely available once you arrive: The **National Park Service Salem Visitor Center,** 2 New Liberty St. (☎ 978/740-1650; www.nps.gov/sama), is open daily from 9am to 5pm from May through October (10am–4pm Wed–Sun, Nov–Apr) and the **Salem Chamber of Commerce,** 265 Essex St., Suite 101 (☎ 978/744-0004; www.salem-chamber.org), is open weekdays from 9am to 5pm. Download or request a visitor's guide from **Destination Salem** (☎ 877/SALEM-MA or ☎ 978/744-3663; www.salem.org).

In October the city goes into Halloween overdrive, with ghost tours, costume balls, haunted houses, a street fair, a parade, and family film nights on the Salem Common. A city-run website, www.hauntedhappenings.org, lists all the options. If you plan to visit during the Halloween season, plan extra time due to traffic and make advance reservations where possible.

The rambling 1668 House of the Seven Gables has a secret staircase and inspired the Nathaniel Hawthorne book of the same name.

grounds, and visitors are invited to poke around the lovely period gardens that overlook the harbor.
⏱ 1½ hr. 115 Derby St. ☎ 978/744-0991. www.7gables.org. $15 adults, $14 seniors, $13 kids 13–18, $10 kids 5–12, free for kids 4 & under. July–Oct daily 10am–7pm; Nov–June daily 10am–5pm. Closed first 2 weeks of Jan & closed Wed–Thurs mid-Jan through mid-Feb.

The easygoing seafood purveyor
7⃣ Sea Level Oyster Bar offers local brews, harbor views, and open-air dining in warmer months. 94 Wharf St. ☎ 978/741-0555. www.sealeveloysterbar.com. $$–$$$.

Plymouth

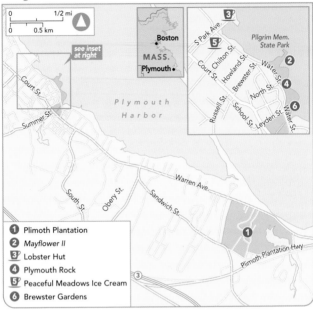

1 Plimoth Plantation
2 *Mayflower II*
3 Lobster Hut
4 Plymouth Rock
5 Peaceful Meadows Ice Cream
6 Brewster Gardens

Most grade school students in the U.S. take part in Thanksgiving pageants and end up remembering *something* about Plymouth: the Pilgrims and their belt-buckle hats. The *Mayflower* ship. That Rock where they landed. Refreshingly, Plymouth honors its history but isn't trapped in the past—it's a lively community with a lot of historic attractions. START: **Take I-93 south and merge onto Route 3 south. To go directly to Plimoth Plantation, take Exit 4. To go straight to Pilgrim Memorial State Park, take Exit 6A (Route 44 east). If it isn't rush hour, the trip from Boston takes about an hour.**

1 ★★ kids Plimoth Plantation
A re-creation of a 1627 village, Plimoth Plantation approximates the conditions in the early days of the little community, which was settled in 1620 (plans are underway to commemorate 400 years in 2020). Visitors wander the village, stepping into homes and gardens constructed with careful attention to historic detail. Re-enactors and educators assume the personalities of original community members, and they take their roles seriously—they will give mystified reactions to questions about bathrooms or queries from women about cooking techniques (they'll ask a male beside her, "doesn't your wife know how to cook?"). Residents spend their days framing houses, shearing sheep, preserving foodstuffs, and cooking over open hearths, all as it was done in the 1600s. Visitors are

Plymouth: Practical Matters

Driving to Plymouth is much easier than taking public transit. **MBTA** commuter rail (☎ 800/392-6100 or ☎ 617/222-3200; www.mbta.com) from Boston's South Station serves Cordage Park, north of downtown Plymouth. The local bus (☎ 800/483-2500; www.gatra.org) finishes up the trip, although it doesn't run on Sunday. There's a seasonal **visitor center** at 130 Water St. (☎ 800/872-1620 or ☎ 508/747-7525), across from Town Pier. Information is available year-round from **Destination Plymouth** (☎ 800/USA-1620 or ☎ 508/747-7533; www.seeplymouth.com).

invited to join some activities—planting, witnessing a trial, visiting a wedding party. A **Wampanoag Homesite** depicts how 17th-century Native People would have lived. Staff here are not actors: They are all either Wampanoag or from other Native Nations. *Mayflower II* ❷, the Plantation's full-scale reproduction of the tall ship that brought the Pilgrims to these shores, is normally located 3 miles up the coast in Pilgrim Memorial State Park at State Pier. It's undergoing a restoration at Mystic Seaport, in Connecticut, and will return in 2019. ⏱ *3 hr. 137 Warren Ave. (Rte. 3).* ☎ *508/746-1622. www.plimoth.org. Admission (good for 2 consecutive days) $28 adults, $26 seniors, $16 kids 6–12, kids 5 & under free. Plimoth*

Plantation & Waterfront Exhibit or Plimoth Grist Mill admission $31 adults, $28 seniors, $19.95 kids 6–12, free for kids 5 & under. Late Mar to Nov daily 9am–5pm. Closed Dec to mid-Mar.

❷ ★ **kids** *Mayflower II* The full-scale reproduction of the vessel that brought the Pilgrims to America in 1620 is just 106½ feet long—and it transported 102 passengers and some 30 crew members on the perilous voyage from England. The ship, which can be boarded by visitors, normally is berthed in the harbor at the small Pilgrim Memorial State Park. Until 2019, however, it's in Connecticut, undergoing renovations (which can be followed online at www.plimoth.org/mayflowerII-blog). Until it returns, a waterfront

Costumed re-enactors at Plimoth Plantation mend a fence as they would have in the 1600s.

Actors aboard Mayflower II *describe the Pilgrims' journey and experience.*

exhibit called *Should I Stay Or Should I Go?* stands in its place, asking visitors to consider what it would it be like to leave everything one knows behind for an unknown world. ① ½ hr. *Pilgrim Memorial State Park, State Pier, 79 Water St.* ☎ *508/746-1622. www.plimoth.org.*

The deck of ③ **Lobster Hut** overlooking Plymouth Harbor is the place to be in Plymouth. *25 Town Wharf (off Water St.).* ☎ *508/746-2270. $–$$.*

④ ★★ **kids Plymouth Rock** Tradition tells us that the original Plymouth Rock was the landing place of the *Mayflower* passengers in 1620. From a hunk that was once 15 feet long and 3 feet wide, the boulder has shrunk to about half its original size due to several relocations and the chipping away by souvenir hunters. In 1867, the rock wound up here, perched at tide level on the peaceful shore and now overseen by the Massachusetts Department of Conservation & Recreation. It's a model attraction: easy to understand, quick to visit, and unexpectedly affecting. ① 10 min. *Pilgrim Memorial State Park, 79 Water St.* ☎ *508/747-5360. www.mass.gov/dcr. Daily 24 hr.*

A family business that dates to 1962, ⑤ **Peaceful Meadows Ice**

Cream is a tasty place to refuel. Take your ice cream (fresh peach, perhaps, if your timing is right) to our final stop. *170 Water St., opposite Town Wharf.* ☎ *508/746-2362. www.peacefulmeadows.com. $.*

⑥ ★ **kids Brewster Gardens** Backtrack along Water Street to wind down at this lovely park, on the site of the garden of an original settler, Elser William Brewster. Settle in to enjoy the greenery, or follow Town Brook up the hill to Jenney Pond, where a waterwheel powers the **Plimoth Grist Mill,** a working mill that's a reproduction of a 1636 corn grinder. It's managed by **Plimoth Plantation** ① and includes a gift shop. ① 1 hr. *Water & Leyden sts.* ☎ *508/830-4095.* ●

Plymouth Rock, on which passengers of the Mayflower *set foot after arriving from England in 1620.*

The Savvy Traveler

Before You Go

Tourist Offices

The **Greater Boston Convention & Visitors Bureau** (☎ 888/SEE-BOSTON or ☎ 617/536-4100; www.bostonusa.com) has two visitor information centers: inside the Copley Place mall at 100 Huntington Avenue and inside the Boston Common at 139 Tremont St. (at West St.). The **Massachusetts Office of Travel and Tourism** (☎ 800/227-MASS or ☎ 617/973-8500; www.massvacation.com) has good regional information on its website.

The Best Times to Go

Conventions, special events, and school vacations make Boston busy virtually year-round. Late June through and August is family vacation season, with large crowds at most attractions. September to early November is back-to-school time and coincides with fall foliage and cooler weather, giving the city the hum of new beginnings. April through early June has smaller crowds. The slowest season is January through March, and many hotels offer deals, especially on weekends.

Special Events

FEBRUARY. Super Bowl Sunday (www.nfl.com/super-bowl) decides the National Football League championship—it's the biggest football game of the year. There's no guarantee that the New England Patriots will be playing, but the odds are good: Between 2002 and 2018, the team went to the big game eight times—and won five of them.

Previous page: The T subway station at Copley Square.

APRIL. The third Monday of April is **Patriots' Day,** a Massachusetts-only holiday that commemorates the events of April 18 and 19, 1775, when the Revolutionary War began. Ceremonies take place in Boston's North End at the **Old North Church** (☎ 617/523-6676; www.oldnorth.com) and the **Paul Revere House** (☎ 617/523-2338; www.paulreverehouse.org). Reenactments take place in suburban **Lexington,** where a skirmish breaks out on the field now known as the Battle Green, and in **Concord,** where hostilities rage at the **North Bridge.** Consult the **Battle Road Committee** (www.battleroad.org) or contact the **Lexington Chamber of Commerce** (☎ 781/862-2480; www.lexingtonchamber.org) or the **Concord Chamber of Commerce** (☎ 978/369-3120; www.concordchamberofcommerce.org) for information. For sporting fans, Patriots' Day is known as **"Marathon Monday"** for the running of the **Boston Marathon** (www.baa.org). One of the oldest and most famous 26.2-mile races in the world, it begins in Hopkinton, Massachusetts, and ends at Boston's Copley Square. Elite women start at 9:30am and elite men at 10am, which means they start arriving on city streets around 11:30am. **Independent Film Festival Boston** (www.iffboston.org) in late April and early May is the biggest and most important film festival in the area. Movies screen at the Brattle in Harvard Square and the Somerville Theatre. IFFBoston also puts on screenings throughout the year.

MAY. Lilac Sunday is held at the **Arnold Arboretum** (☎ 617/524-1718; www.arboretum.harvard.edu) on the second or third weekend of

Useful Websites

- **MBTA** (Massachusetts Bay Transportation Authority's route maps and schedules for subway, trolley, bus, and commuter-rail, with a trip planner feature): www.mbta.com
- **Boston.com** (news from the *Boston Globe*): www.boston.com
- **Greater Boston Convention & Visitors Bureau:** www.bostonusa.com and www.twitter.com/bostoninsider
- **National Park Service:** www.nps.gov (search for "Boston")
- **Boston-to-English Dictionary** (comical guide to Boston's vocabulary, way of pronouncing words, and unique grammatical constructs): www.universalhub.com/glossary

May. The collection is among the largest in North America. It's the only day of the year that the arboretum allows picnicking. On **Mother's Day,** the second Sunday in May, the **Duckling Parade** (www.friendsofthepublicgarden.org) is a sweet, uniquely Boston event. It celebrates Robert McCloskey's children's book *Make Way for Ducklings* with a parade for young children. They march (or toddle) dressed as ducklings from the Boston Common into the Public Garden. **Boston Calling Music Festival** (www.bostoncalling.com) is a 3-day music and comedy fest held at Harvard's Athletic Complex in Allston. The 2018 lineup included musicians Eminem, Jack White, Khalid, and Belly, and comedian Jenny Slate.

JUNE. **Boston Pride Week** (☎ 617/262-9405; www.bostonpride.org) takes place at the beginning of June and includes a festival, a concert, block parties, and the largest gay-pride parade in New England. Additional Pride events are held in February (Black Pride), April (Latinx Pride), and May (Youth Pride).

JULY. **Boston Harborfest** (☎ 617/439-7700; www.bostonharborfest.com), is the city's 6-day party

leading up to the **Fourth of July** concert and fireworks. Events include historical reenactments, boat tours, harborside concerts, and a Chowderfest. July 4th ends with a beloved tradition, the **Boston Pops Fireworks Spectacular** (www.july4th.org). The orchestra plays at the Hatch Shell amphitheater on the Charles River Esplanade, and spectators spread out along both banks of the river and on the Longfellow and Mass Ave. bridges. Fireworks are set off from river barges. Later in the month, the **Bastille Day Party** hosted by the French Cultural Center (☎ 617/912-0400 www.frenchculturalcenter.org) takes over Marlborough Street in Back Bay for a nighttime celebration of Francophone cultures. It sells out so buy tickets in advance.

AUGUST. The North End is home to the **Italian-American feasts** that dominate weekends from late July through August. The street fairs feature live music, dancing, carnival food, and lively crowds of locals and out-of-towners. The two biggest are the **Fisherman's Feast** (www.fishermansfeast.com) in mid-August and the **Feast of St. Anthony** (www.saintanthonysfeast.

BOSTON'S AVERAGE MONTHLY TEMPERATURES

	JAN	FEB	MAR	APR	MAY	JUNE
High (°F)	37	39	46	56	67	77
High (°C)	3	4	8	13	19	25
Low (°F)	22	24	32	41	50	62
Low (°C)	–6	–4	0	5	10	17

	JULY	AUG	SEPT	OCT	NOV	DEC
High (°F)	82	80	73	62	52	42
High (°C)	28	27	23	17	11	6
Low (°F)	66	65	57	46	38	28
Low (°C)	19	18	14	8	3	–2

com)—celebrating its 100th anniversary in 2019—the following weekend.

SEPTEMBER. Open Studios (www.boston.gov/departments/arts-and-culture/boston-open-studios-coalition) are opportunities to visit artists in their studios and buy art from them directly. In Boston, 11 neighborhoods host special open studio weekends, providing visitors a great excuse to explore a new neighborhood. Two of the most established are put on by **Jamaica Plain Arts Council** (www.facebook.com/JPOpenStudios) in September and **Fort Point Arts Community** (www.fortpointarts.org) in May and October. Up in Somerville, **Fluff Festival** (www.flufffestival.com) celebrates the marshmallow spread, which was invented in the city in 1917. There's music, Fluff-themed games, and of course Fluff treats.

OCTOBER. Boston Book Festival (☎ 857/259-6999; www.bostonbookfest.org) takes place in Copley Square and features author panels and outdoor exhibitors. The **HONK! festival** of activist street bands (www.honkfest.org) brings the sounds of New Orleans, Klezmer, Afrobeat, and punk to Somerville for a weekend of free outdoor performance and a parade down Massachusetts Avenue. **Head of the Charles Regatta**

(☎ 617/868-6200; www.hocr.org), on the third weekend of October, draws some 10,000 athletes from around the world to the Charles River in Cambridge for the 2-day rowing competition; tens of thousands of fans line the shore and the bridges. Fifteen miles north in Salem (p 150), **Haunted Happenings** (☎ 877/SALEM-MA; www.hauntedhappenings.org) lasts all month, leading up to Halloween on October 31. There are haunted houses, walking tours, fortune-tellers, and a built-in excuse to dress up in costume.

NOVEMBER–DECEMBER. Boston's holiday season begins in late November on the day after Thanksgiving, when **Boston Ballet** kicks off its annual performances of *The Nutcracker* (☎ 617/695-6955; www.bostonballet.org). At Harvard's Sanders Theatre, the **Christmas Revels** show (☎ 617/972-8300; www.revels.org) is a multicultural celebration of the winter solstice, illuminating the customs of a different culture each year. Buy tickets to both early. **First Night First Day celebration** (www.firstnightboston.org) is an arts-oriented family-friendly New Year's celebration, and includes music performances, ice sculptures, a parade, and New Year's Eve fireworks.

The Weather
New England weather is famously changeable—variations from day to day and even hour to hour can be enormous (on one strange day in January 2018 the temperature went from 61 down to 19). Spring has moderate temperatures but often doesn't settle in until early May. Summers are hot, especially in July and August, and can be uncomfortably humid. Fall is when you're most likely to catch a run of dry, sunny days and cool nights. Winters are cold and often snowy—a warm coat and waterproof boots are essential.

Cellphones
Check with your phone company about using your phone in the U.S. if you're traveling from abroad, and about roaming fees. Short-term data plans may make financial sense; ask your provider for options. Many travelers use Web-based services such as **Skype** (www.skype.com) and **WhatsApp** (www.whatsapp.com) to make free calls.

Getting There

By Plane
Boston's **Logan International Airport** (airport code BOS) is in East Boston, 3 miles (4.8km) from downtown and across the harbor. For information, including real-time flight arrivals and departures, go to **www.massport.com/logan-airport**. Free Wi-Fi is available throughout the airport.

Getting to & from the Airport
General Info: Massachusetts Port Authority, or **MassPort** (☎ 800/235-6426; www.massport.com/logan-airport), coordinates airport transportation. Public Service information booths are located near baggage claim on the first floor arrivals level of every terminal.

Public Transit: The Silver Line SL1 bus stops at each airport terminal and runs to downtown Boston's South Station, which has connections to the Red Line subway and the commuter rail to the southern suburbs. The 20-minute ride is free and includes a transfer to the Red Line. The other public transport option is to take the free airport shuttle bus (either Route 22, 33, 55, or 66) to the stop "MBTA Blue Line" to pick up the subway on the Blue Line. The Blue Line runs daily from approximately 6am to 12:20am. Subway fare is $2.75 with a paper CharlieTicket from a vending machine. See p 162 for details about the subway system.

Taxis/Lyft/Uber: Taxis are available at each terminal in the airport. Between airport fees and the initial drop the starting price is about $10; the total fare to downtown runs $25 to $45. As of 2017 there are designated areas at Logan for pick up by **Lyft** (www.lyft.com) and **Uber** (www.uber.com) drivers. Travelers using one of these "Transportation Network Companies" should look for the designated pickup areas on the lower level (Arrivals) and the sign "App Ride/TNC." The fare will include a $3.25 airport fee.

Shuttle Vans: The Logan Airport website lists private van services that serve local hotels. One-way prices start at $15 per person and can include extra fees. Check your hotel for the best option.

Ferries & Water Taxis: The Harbor Express ferry trip from Logan to Long Wharf on the downtown waterfront takes about 7 minutes and costs $18.50 one-way. The free no. 66 shuttle bus connects airport terminals to the Logan ferry dock. As well, **Boston Harbor Cruises Water Taxi** (☎ 617/227-4320; www.boston harborcruises.com/water-taxi) and **Rowes Wharf Water Transport** (☎ 617/406-8584; www.rowes wharfwatertransport.com) serve the airport, the downtown waterfront, and other points around the harbor. Leaving the airport, ask the no. 66 shuttle-bus driver to radio ahead for water-taxi pickup.

By Car
Three major highways converge in Boston. The **I-90,** also known as the Massachusetts Turnpike or "Mass. Pike," is an east-west toll road. **I-93/U.S. 1** goes north. **I-93/Route 3,** the Southeast Expressway, heads south and toward Cape Cod.

The **I-95** (Massachusetts Rte. 128) is a beltway about 11 miles from downtown that connects Boston to highways in Rhode Island, Connecticut, and New York to the south, and New Hampshire and Maine to the north.

Approaches to Cambridge include **Storrow Drive** and **Memorial Drive,** which run along either side of the Charles River. Storrow has a Harvard Square exit that leads across the Anderson Bridge to John F. Kennedy Street and into the square. "Mem Drive" intersects with JFK Street, although only northbound traffic can make the turn toward the square.

By Train & Bus
Boston has three transportation centers. The biggest is **South Station,** at 700 Atlantic Ave. It is a nexus of Amtrak trains, MBTA commuter trains, bus lines, and stops on the subway's Red and Silver Lines. The two other centers are **Back Bay Station,** at 145 Dartmouth St., and **North Station,** at 135 Causeway St. **Amtrak** (☎ 800/USA-RAIL; www.amtrak.com) serves all three stations, each of which is also an MBTA subway stop. **The South Station Bus Terminal** (www.south-station.net) is at 700 Atlantic Ave. and adjoins the train station.

Getting Around

On Foot
Walking is the way to go if you can manage it. Boston is nearly flat, and even the tallest hills aren't too steep.

By Bike
Boston has a bike-sharing program (www.thehubway.com). It started in 2011 as "Hubway" and in 2018 was rebranded **Blue Bike.** The system has 1,600 bikes at 180 stations across Boston and in neighboring Cambridge, Brookline, and Somerville. Helmets are not included so bring your own. A 24-hour pass,

with unlimited 30-minute trips, is $8, and a 72-hour pass is $15. It's a year-round service, with most stations open in the winter months.

By Public Transportation
The **Massachusetts Bay Transportation Authority,** or MBTA (☎ 800/392-6100 or ☎ 617/222-3200; www.mbta.com), runs subways, trolleys, buses, and ferries in Boston and many suburbs, as well as the commuter rail, which extends as far south as Providence, Rhode Island.

The stored-value fare system is complex (and will be changing in 2020 to an all-electronic payment system). For now, travelers have the option of using either paper CharlieTickets or plastic CharlieCards or cash (on buses and above-ground Green Line subway stops only). CharlieTickets are easier to find—they're available from kiosks at every station and every airport terminal—but users pay more. With a CharlieTicket, the subway fare is $2.75, the bus fare $2. Users can load up a CharlieTicket with either enough money just for one fare or, say, $20 to cover several rides. With a plastic CharlieCard—available from employees who staff most downtown subway stations—subway riders pay $2.25, bus passengers $1.70, and transfers are either free or less expensive than with a CharlieTicket. As with the CharlieTicket, users can load and reload a CharlieCard with as much money as they'd like. Children age 11 and younger ride free (up to 2 children per adult).

Cards can also be loaded with 1-Day, 7-Day, or monthly passes. A 1-Day pass is $12, a 7-Day pass is $21.25, and a monthly pass (calendar month) is $84.50.

To use the plastic CharlieCard, tap the target at a subway turnstile or on the bus. To use the paper CharlieTicket, insert the ticket into the slot on the turnstile or at the front of the bus and then remove the ticket to keep.

The subway system is called "the T" and consists of the Red, Green, Blue, and Orange lines. The Silver Line is a bus that travels both above ground and underground and is part of the subway system. The commuter rail to the suburbs is purple on system maps and sometimes called the Purple Line. Service begins around 5:15am and ends around 1am. The **MBTA trip planner** (www.mbta.com/trip-planner) provides route options. Park Street station, which is a stop on both the Red and Green lines, is the center of the network. Train tracks are labeled as either "inbound" (toward Park St. and the center of the city) or "outbound" (away from Park St. and the city center).

Buses and "trackless trolleys" (buses with electric antennae) travel through the city and to many suburbs. The Silver Line has two (unconnected) sections. Riders on the Washington Street branches (SL4 and SL5) pay bus fares; riders on the Waterfront branches (SL1 and SL2), pay subway fares.

Commuter-rail tickets are available at stations and on the trains, with a surcharge for on-board purchases.

The Boston Harbor water shuttle (☎ **617/227-4321**) is a commuter ferry that connects Long Wharf, near the New England Aquarium, with the Charlestown Navy Yard. The ride takes 10 minutes. The one-way fare is $3.50.

By Taxi / Lyft / Uber

Taxis can be tough to hail on the street. Your best bet is to go to a hotel, since many have cabstands. Both Lyft (www.lyft.com) and Uber (www.uber.com) are active and popular in the city.

By Car

If you drive, using GPS or the app **Waze** (www.waze.com) on a smartphone will help considerably with navigation. Keep in mind that road patterns are often confusing—few sections of the city use a grid system, and many streets are one-way. Street parking is a challenge and a matter of good luck in most parts of Boston. See p 166 for parking information.

Fast Facts

AREA CODES Area codes 617 and 857 serve Boston and several surrounding communities, including Cambridge. To make a call, you must include the area code and dial all 10 digits.

ATMS/CASHPOINTS Check ahead to see if your bank operates any ATMs in Boston. Otherwise, expect to pay a $1.50 to $3 access fee.

BABYSITTERS Some hotels maintain lists of babysitters; check at the front desk or with the concierge. Websites such as Care.com also coordinate services. The going rate in Boston is about $15 an hour.

B&BS **B&B Agency of Boston** (☎ 617/720-3540; www.boston-bnbagency.com) is recommended by the Greater Boston Convention & Visitors Bureau. **Airbnb** (www.airbnb.com/locations/boston) has a large selection of Boston room and properties for rent.

BANKING HOURS Most banks are open weekdays 9am–5pm, and some are open Saturday mornings.

CLIMATE See "The Weather," earlier in this chapter.

CONSULATES & EMBASSIES Embassies are in Washington, D.C. Some consulates have offices in major U.S. cities. The U.S. Department of State maintains a list of embassy websites at www.state.gov/s/cpr/32122.htm. For addresses and phone numbers of embassies in Washington, D.C., call ☎ 202/555-1212 or visit www.usembassy.gov. The State Department also lists foreign consular offices in a PDF: www.state.gov/documents/organization/256839.pdf. They include the **Canadian consulate,** at 3 Copley Place, Suite 400, Boston, MA 02116 (☎ 617/262-3760; www.boston.gc.ca); the **Irish consulate,**

at 535 Boylston St., 5th floor, Boston, MA 02116 (☎ **617/267-9330;** www.dfa.ie/irish-consulate/boston); and the **U.K. consulate,** at 1 Broadway, Cambridge, MA 02142 (☎ **617/245-4500;** www.gov.uk/world/usa).

CUSTOMS National customs agencies strictly regulate what visitors to the United States may bring with them and take home. For details regarding U.S. Customs and Border Protection, consult your nearest U.S. embassy or consulate or visit www.cbp.gov.

DENTISTS The desk staff at your hotel should be able to suggest a dentist. The **Massachusetts Dental Society** (☎ 800/342-8747; www.massdental.org) maintains a searchable database.

DOCTORS The desk staff at your hotel can direct you to a doctor. You can also try the physician referral service at one of the area's many hospitals listed on p 165.

DRINKING LAWS See "Liquor Laws," below.

ELECTRICITY The United States uses 110–120 volts AC (60 cycles). This is the same standard as Canada. Most of Europe, Australia, and New Zealand use 220–240 volts AC (50 cycles). Downward converters that change 220–240 volts to 110–120 volts are difficult to find in the United States, so bring one if you'll need it.

EMBASSIES See "Consulates & Embassies," above.

EMERGENCIES Call ☎ 911 for fire, ambulance, or police. This is a free call from pay phones. The toll-free number for the **Poison Control Center** is ☎ 800/222-1222.

HOLIDAYS Banks, government offices, post offices, and some stores, restaurants, and museums close on the following legal national holidays: January 1 (New Year's Day), the third Monday in January (Martin Luther King, Jr. Day), the third Monday in February (Presidents' Day), the last Monday in May (Memorial Day), July 4 (Independence Day), the first Monday in September (Labor Day), the second Monday in October (Columbus Day), November 11 (Veterans' Day/ Armistice Day), the fourth Thursday in November (Thanksgiving Day), and December 25 (Christmas Day). Also, the Tuesday following the first Monday in November is Election Day and is a federal government holiday in presidential-election years (held every 4 years, next in 2020). In Massachusetts, state offices close for Patriots' Day on the third Monday in April.

HOSPITALS Both **Massachusetts General Hospital,** 55 Fruit St. (☎ 617/726-2000; www.mass general.org), and **Tufts Medical Center,** 800 Washington St. (☎ 617/636-5000; www.tufts medicalcenter.org), are close to downtown. There is a major medical area west of the city on the Boston–Brookline border, which includes **Beth Israel Deaconess Medical Center,** 330 Brookline Ave. (☎ 617/667-7000; www. bidmc.org); **Brigham and Women's Hospital,** 75 Francis St. (☎ 617/ 732-5500; www.brighamandwomens. org); and **Boston Children's Hospital,** 300 Longwood Ave. (☎ 617/ 355-6000; www.childrenshospital. org). In Cambridge, **Mount Auburn Hospital,** 330 Mount Auburn St. (☎ 617/492-3500; www.mount auburnhospital.org) is less than a mile from Harvard Square.

INSURANCE It's a smart idea to get insurance for international travel. To find a policy that fits your needs, head to SquareMouth.com or InsureMyTrip.com. These two marketplace websites only work with well-established insurance companies, and will show you, in 10-seconds-flat, an array of policies.

INTERNET Wireless access is widely available throughout Boston, often for no charge. Many hotels offer terminals in business centers. **FedEx Office** (www.fedexoffice. com) offers free Wi-Fi and rental computer workstations at most branches. Locations include 2 Center Plaza, Government Center (☎ **617/973-9000**) and 10 Post Office Sq., Financial District (☎ **617/482-4400**).

LIQUOR LAWS The legal drinking age in Massachusetts (and the rest of the U.S.) is 21. Many bars, particularly those near college campuses, check the ID of everyone who enters. Last call typically is 30 minutes before closing time—2am by law, although many bars close at 1am. Liquor stores and the liquor sections of other stores are open Monday through Saturday and, in some communities, on Sunday.

MAIL & POSTAGE Domestic postage rates are 35¢ for a postcard and 50¢ for a letter as of January 2018. For international mail, a first-class letter of up to 1 ounce or a postcard costs $1.15. Most post offices are open 7:30am to 5:30pm Monday through Friday and 7:30am to early afternoon on Saturday. The location at 25 Dorchester Ave. (☎ **617/654-5302**), next to South Station, is open 24 hours.

MONEY / TRAVELER'S CHECKS Credit or debit cards are accepted at almost all shops, restaurants, and hotels, but you should always keep some cash on hand for small venues that don't take plastic. International visitors with traveler's checks should carry them denominated in U.S. dollars; foreign-currency checks are often difficult to exchange.

PARKING Most parking spaces in Boston are metered and in operation until at least 6pm (and sometimes 8pm) Monday through Saturday. Meters cost $1.25 to $4 an hour, depending on the neighborhood; as of 2018 the city was testing using "surge rates" for the most popular times in Back Bay and the Seaport District. Pay either at the meter itself with quarters (for older meters) or credit or debit cards (at newer meters). Some spots have pay-and-display kiosks, which accept cash and cards; you affix the receipt to the inside of the car window facing the sidewalk. In neighborhoods where there is resident-only parking there are often some guest spots for nonresidents, usually for 2 hours between 8am and 6pm.

A full day in a garage can be as much as $45, and hourly rates can be high. The large city-run garage under **Boston Common** (☎ 617/954-2098) is bright and well-maintained and costs $28 for up to 10 hours, with cheaper rates nights and weekends. The entrance is at Zero Charles St., between Boylston and Beacon streets heading north. Other options are listed by neighborhood at www.boston-discovery-guide.com/parking-in-boston.html.

PASSPORTS Keep a photocopy of your passport with you or stored digitally (you can email a photo of it to yourself) when you're traveling. If your passport is lost or stolen, having a copy facilitates the reissuing process at a consulate or embassy (p 164).

RESTROOMS Tourist attractions, hotels, department stores, malls, and public buildings have public restrooms. Some restaurants and bars, especially in busy areas, display signs noting that toilets are for the use of their patrons only. Buying a cup of coffee qualifies you as a patron.

SAFETY Boston and Cambridge are generally safe cities, but you should always take the same precautions you would in any other large North American city. Avoid walking alone at night in parks including Boston Common, the Rose Kennedy Greenway, and the Esplanade. Specific areas to be careful in are the Theater District and the side streets around North Station. Public transportation is busy and safe, but service stops between 12:30am and 1am.

SMOKING Massachusetts law bans smoking in all workplaces, including restaurants, bars, and clubs. Some buildings forbid smoking within a 10- to 25-foot radius of the entrance. Recreational use of marijuana became legal in Massachusetts in 2016.

TAXES There's a 6.25% state sales tax in Massachusetts. Exempt categories include groceries, prescription drugs, and clothing that costs less than $175. The hotel tax is 14.95% in Boston and Cambridge.

TELEPHONES For directory assistance or information, dial ☎ **411.** Pay phones are no longer generally available.

TIPPING In hotels, tip bellhops $1 per bag and tip the housekeeping staff $5 per day. Tip the doorman or concierge only for a specific service (for example, calling a cab for you). Tip the valet-parking attendant $1 or $2. In restaurants, bars, and nightclubs, tip service staff 15% to 20% of the check, tip bartenders 15%, and tip checkroom attendants $1 per garment. Tip cab drivers 15% of the fare, tip skycaps at airports $1 per bag, and tip hairdressers and barbers 15% to 20%.

TOILETS See "Restrooms," above.

TOURIST INFORMATION OFFICES
Faneuil Hall Visitor Center

(☎ 617/242-5642; www.nps.gov/ bost; daily 9am–5pm), at Faneuil Hall Marketplace off Congress Street near North Street, is managed by the National Park Service. **Boston Common Visitor Information Center,** inside the Common at 148 Tremont St. (Mon–Fri 8:30am–5pm, Sat 9am–5pm) and **Copley Place Visitor Information Desk** inside the Copley Place Mall at the Dartmouth Street entrance, 100 Huntington Ave. (Mon–Fri 9am–5pm, Sat–Sun 10am–6pm) are both run by **Greater Boston Convention & Visitors Bureau** (☎ 888/SEE-BOSTON or ☎ 617/536-4100; www.bostonusa.com).

TRANSIT INFO **Massachusetts Bay Transportation Authority,** or MBTA, runs the subway and bus system, known as the **"T"**; see p 162. **Massachusetts Port Authority** coordinates airport transportation; see p 161.

TRAVELERS WITH DISABILITIES While Boston is compliant with accessibility guidelines of the Americans with Disabilities Act and the Commonwealth's own rules, **some of Boston's historic sites have limited accessibility** for wheelchairs. The National Park Service lists some of the most popular sites with notes about access at www.nps.gov/bost/ planyourvisit/index.htm. Most **MBTA** transit stations and all buses are accessible to people with disabilities (☎ 800/392-6100 or ☎ 617/222-3200; www.mbta. com/accessibility). When there's snow, wheelchair travel anywhere, including bus stops, can be difficult. **Boston Cab** (☎ 617/536-5010; www.bostoncab.us) has wheelchair-accessible vans. At Logan airport, transportation attendants at the taxi stands will help visitors find an accessible vehicle.

Boston: A Brief History

1630 English Puritans looking to escape religious persecution and heartened by the establishment of Plymouth Colony 10 years earlier sail to the New World. With a royal charter in hand, they establish the Massachusetts Bay Colony on the shores of what they name Boston.

1635 Boston Latin School, America's first public school, opens.

1636 Harvard College, the nation's first institution of higher learning, is founded in Cambridge.

1638 America's first printing press is established in Cambridge.

1639 The General Court of Massachusetts designates Richard Fairbanks' Boston tavern as the colonies' first official repository mail station.

1692 The Salem witch trials take place 16 miles north of Boston, accusing men and women of witchcraft and resulting in 20 executions.

1770 On March 5, five colonists are killed by British Army soldiers outside what is now the Old State House; the incident quickly becomes known as the Boston Massacre.

1773 In a protest against taxation, colonists dump 342 chests of tea into the harbor from three British ships, in an act known as the Boston Tea Party. This ramps up talk of war on both sides.

1775 On April 18, rebel colonists Paul Revere and William Dawes spread the word that British troops are marching toward Lexington and Concord, 16 miles northwest of Boston. The next day, "the shot heard round the world" is fired and the Battles of Lexington and Concord and the Siege of Boston ensue, launching the American Revolutionary War. On June 17, the British win the Battle of Bunker Hill but suffer heavy casualties.

1776 On March 17, royal troops evacuate Boston by ship after General George Washington and the Continental Army move into Dorchester Heights and position cannons to face the Boston harbor. On July 18, the Declaration of Independence—adopted in Philadelphia 2 weeks earlier—is read from the balcony of the Old State House.

1793 The first stagecoach between Boston and Cambridge opens.

1811 Massachusetts General Hospital is built.

1813 As the industrial revolution begins to shift Massachusetts' economy from agriculture, fishing, and maritime shipping into manufacturing, Francis Cabot Lowell cofounds the Boston Manufacturing Company, a textile and mill company that introduced the power loom.

1831 Newspaper editor William Lloyd Garrison publishes the first issue of his anti-slavery newspaper, *The Liberator,* in Boston.

1876 The Museum of Fine Arts opens in a Sturgis and Brigham–designed building in Copley Square.

1872 The Great Fire, one of the worst in American history, kills 13 to 30 people (different sources cite different numbers) and destroys 776 buildings. It consumes the entire area that makes up today's Financial District, from State Street to Summer Street down to the harbor.

1876 Alexander Graham Bell—who opened a School of Vocal Physiology for teachers of the deaf in in Boston 1872 and then became a professor of the mechanism of speech at Boston University's—invents the telephone. His famous words "Mr. Watson, come here I want to see you" are said at his workshop at 109 Court St., where the Government Center T is today.

1881 The Boston Symphony Orchestra is founded.

1887 More than 20 companies with some 8,000 horses are providing horsecar service around Boston.

1888 Helen Keller, future disability advocate, begins her studies at Perkins School for the Blind, the first school for the blind in the U.S.

1894 The original Mother Church for Christian Science, a religious movement founded by Mary Baker Eddy, opens on Massachusetts Avenue.

1895 The Boston Public Library opens on Copley Square in a "palace for the people" designed by architect Charles Follen McKim. Artist John Singer Sargent begins painting his "Triumph of Religion" murals inside the library.

1897 The first subway tunnel in the United States opens—the stretch is still in use on the Green Line, from Government Center down to Boylston Street.

1897 The first Boston Marathon is run.

1903 Arts patron Isabella Stewart Gardner opens her opulent museum, built in the style of a Venetian palace, displaying her vast collection of paintings, sculptures, and tapestries.

1909 The Museum of Fine Arts moves to its current location in the Fenway in a Beaux Arts building designed by Boston architect Guy Lowell.

1912 Fenway Park, home of the Boston Red Sox baseball team, opens on April 20.

1918 The Red Sox win the baseball World Series—and subsequently launch a dry spell that would not be broken until 2004.

1919 The Great Molasses Flood kills 21 people and injures 150 in the North End after a 50-foot tall molasses storage tank bursts and sends a wave of molasses as high as 25 feet through the streets.

1930 Arthur Fiedler begins what will become a 50-year tenure as conductor of the Boston Pops orchestra, organizing the first Fourth of July concert on the Charles River Esplanade and ushering the Pops into its status as the most recorded orchestra in history.

1930s The Great Depression devastates what remains of New England's industrial base.

1942 A fire at the post-Prohibition Cocoanut Grove nightclub in Bay Village kills 492 people. The deadliest nightclub fire in history, it leads to new fire codes across the country and advances in the medical treatment of burn victims.

1946 Boston's First Congressional District sends 29-year-old John F. Kennedy to Congress.

1948 Polaroid, founded in Cambridge in 1937, introduces the world's first instant camera, invented by company cofounder Edwin Land.

1954 Oral contraceptives get their first clinical trials at Boston Lying-In Hospital, now part of Brigham and Women's, thanks to women's health advocate Margaret Sanger, funder Katharine Dexter McCormick, and Dr. John Rock, who conducted the study.

1954 The world's first organ transplant, of a kidney, takes place at Brigham Hospital.

1957 The Boston Celtics win the National Basketball Association championship.

1958 Much of Boston's immigrant-heavy West End neighborhood is demolished between 1958 and 1960 in an urban renewal project that ushers in a new highway, housing and commercial buildings, and city offices at what's now Government Center.

1959 Construction begins on the Prudential Center, setting in place a transformation of the city skyline.

1960 John F. Kennedy, with his broad Boston accent, is elected 35th President of the United States, bringing new attention to the city.

1963 Julia Child's cooking show "The French Chef" debuts on Boston TV station WGBH.

1964 The Massachusetts Bay Transportation Authority, or "T," is voted into law, the first combined regional transit system in the United States.

1966 Edward Brooke—who two years earlier became the first African American to both hold statewide office in Massachusetts and serve as any state's attorney general—becomes the first African American popularly elected to the U.S. Senate.

1967 Kathrine Switzer, registered as "K. V. Switzer," becomes the first woman to run and finish the Boston Marathon with a race number.

1968 The night after the assassination of civil-rights leader Martin Luther King Jr., musician James Brown, the "Godfather of Soul," helps calm emotional Bostonians through his concert at the Boston Garden, which is broadcast live on TV.

1969 Students protesting the Vietnam War occupy University Hall at Harvard.

1972 Jonathan Richman and the Modern Lovers release "Roadrunner," a pop song celebrating the back roads of Massachusetts. Starting in 2013 there will be ongoing campaigns to make it the official state song.

1973 Boston rock band Aerosmith issues its debut album, including the top-ten single "Dream On."

1974 Twenty years after the U.S. Supreme Court made school segregation illegal, race-based busing of Boston children to schools outside of their neighborhoods begins. The integration plan sparks criticism and sometimes violent protest by students and adults.

1975 Boston hosts the nation's first First Night event on New Year's Eve, bringing together musicians and artists for a family-friendly daylong celebration.

1976 Faneuil Hall Marketplace, which had been a hub of commerce in the 1800s but become dilapidated by the mid-1900s, is renovated, changing the tenor of Boston's downtown.

1976 USS *Constitution,* launched in 1797, leads a parade of tall ships up Boston Harbor for Operation Sail, part of the U.S. bicentennial celebrations.

1980 Composer and Hollywood musical royalty John Williams succeeds Arthur Fiedler as conductor of the Boston Pops.

1982 Boston-based sitcom "Cheers," set in a bar "where everybody knows your name," debuts on TV and begins an 11-year run.

1983 New Edition, a boy band from Roxbury inspired by the Jackson Five, releases its first album, *Candy Girl.* The title track goes to number one on the American R&B singles chart and the UK singles chart.

1987 Funding for the massive Central Artery/Third Harbor Tunnel Project, known colloquially as the "Big Dig," is approved.

1988 Strong regional economic growth thanks to a new wave of high-tech companies and financial services in Boston and along Route 128 is dubbed the "Massachusetts Miracle." It's touted by Massachusetts Governor Michael Dukakis in his campaign for the U.S. Presidency.

1989 After success producing New Edition, Maurice Starr starts another Boston boy band, this time with white teenagers. With "I'll Be Loving You (Forever)," New Kids on the Block goes to No. 1 on the Billboard Hot 100 Singles chart.

1990 Thieves make off with 13 paintings from the Gardner Museum in the dark of night. Included are works by Rembrandt, Vermeer, and Degas, together worth more than $500 million. It is the single largest property theft in the world.

1993 Thomas Menino is elected mayor, a job he will hold until 2014, making him the city's longest-serving mayor.

1995 The first complete piece of the Big Dig, the Ted Williams Tunnel, opens. It's named after a baseball great who played his entire career with the Red Sox.

1997 *Good Will Hunting,* by locals Matt Damon and Ben Affleck, is released. The friends win an Academy Award for their screenplay.

1999 School busing ends after the Boston School Committee votes to eliminate race as a factor in deciding which schools its 64,000 students will attend.

2001 On September 11, planes flying out of Boston's Logan Airport are hijacked by terrorists. They crash into New York's World Trade Center, killing 2,753 people in the immediate attack.

2001 Preeminent chef Lydia Shire takes over the landmark Locke-Ober, a relic of Boston's Brahmin history—and a restaurant that had prohibited women from its dining room for 97 years.

2002 The New England Patriots win the football team's first Super Bowl.

2003 The Massachusetts Supreme Judicial Court becomes the first state supreme court in the United States to rule that same-sex couples have the legal right to marry.

2003 The Leonard P. Zakim Bunker Hill Bridge, the signature structure of the Big Dig and a symbol of 21st-century Boston, opens to traffic. Demolition of the elevated Central Artery begins.

2004 As a result of the 2003 state court decision, Massachusetts becomes the first U.S. state to issue marriage licenses to same-sex couples.

2004 The Red Sox win the baseball World Series for the first time since 1918, breaking the 86-year "curse of the Bambino."

2006 The Institute of Contemporary Art opens the first new art museum in Boston in nearly a century, a dramatic waterfront structure that accelerates a revival of the Seaport District.

2008 The Celtics win the National Basketball Association title, breaking a 22-year dry spell.

2008 Massachusetts voters decriminalize marijuana possession.

2009 Boston's most eligible bachelor, football quarterback Tom Brady, goes off the market when he marries Brazilian supermodel Gisele Bündchen.

2009 Edward "Ted" Kennedy, the liberal "Lion of the Senate" who represented Massachusetts in Congress for 46 years, dies.

2011 The Boston Bruins win the Stanley Cup, after 39 years without a National Hockey League title.

2011 Mobster James "Whitey" Bulger, head of the vicious Winter Hill Gang and one of the most wanted fugitives in America, is arrested in California after 16 years on the lam.

2012 Fenway Park celebrates its 100th birthday and status as the oldest Major League Baseball stadium in the U.S., hosting an open house to the public.

2013 Two bombs are detonated near the Boston Marathon finish line, killing spectators Krystle Campbell, Lingzi Lu, and Martin Richard and injuring another 264 people. MIT campus police officer Sean Collier is killed 3 days later by the bombers. A midnight gunfight in Watertown ends with one bomber dead and the other in hiding, sending Boston into an essential lockdown. Thousands of law enforcement officers, SWAT teams, and armored vehicles pour into Watertown. The suspect is found and arrested at the end of a tense and surreal day.

2014 Martin "Marty" Walsh takes office as Boston's mayor.

2015 The Head of The Charles Regatta, the largest 2-day regatta in the world, celebrates its 50th anniversary. Nearly 10,000 athletes from across the globe compete.

Websites

Airlines Serving Logan Airport

AER LINGUS
www.aerlingus.com
AEROMEXICO
www.aeromexico.com
AIR CANADA
www.aircanada.com
AIR FRANCE
www.airfrance.com
ALASKA AIRLINES
www.alaskaair.com
ALITALIA
www.alitalia.com
AMERICAN AIRLINES
www.aa.com
AVIANCA
www.avianca.com
AZORES AIRLINES (SATA)
www.azoresairlines.pt
BRITISH AIRWAYS
www.britishairways.com
CAPE AIR
www.capeair.com
CATHAY PACIFIC
www.cathaypacific.com
COPA AIRLINES
www.copaair.com
DELTA AIR LINES
www.delta.com
EL AL
www.elal.com
EMIRATES
www.emirates.com

HAINAN AIRLINES
www.hainanairlines.com
IBERIA
www.iberia.com
ICELANDAIR
www.icelandair.com
JAPAN AIRLINES
www.ar.jal.com
JETBLUE
www.jetblue.com
LATAM
www.latam.com
LEVEL
www.flylevel.com
LUFTHANSA
www.lufthansa.com
NORWEGIAN
www.norwegian.com
PENAIR
www.penair.com
PORTER
www.flyporter.com
PRIMERA AIR
www.primeraair.com
QATAR AIRWAYS
www.qatarairways.com
SCANDINAVIAN AIRLINES
www.flysas.com
SOUTHWEST
www.southwest.com
SPIRIT
www.spirit.com
SUN COUNTRY AIRLINES
www.suncountry.com

SWISS AIR
www.swiss.com

TACV
www.flytacv.com

TAP PORTUGAL
www.flytap.com

THOMAS COOK AIRLINES
www.thomascookairlines.com

TURKISH AIRLINES
www.turkishairlines.com

UNITED AIRLINES
www.united.com

VIRGIN AMERICA
www.virginamerica.com

VIRGIN ATLANTIC
www.virgin-atlantic.com

WESTJET
www.westjet.com

WOW AIR
www.wowair.us

Car-Rental Companies Available at Logan Airport

ADVANTAGE
www.advantage.com

ALAMO
www.alamo.com

AVIS
www.avis.com

BUDGET
www.budget.com

DOLLAR
www.dollar.com

ENTERPRISE
www.enterprise.com

E-Z RENT-A-CAR
www.e-zrentacar.com

HERTZ
www.hertz.com

NATIONAL
www.nationalcar.com

PAYLESS
www.paylesscar.com

THRIFTY
www.thrifty.com

ZIPCAR
www.zipcar.com

Major Hotel & Motel Chains in & near Boston

BEST WESTERN
www.bestwestern.com

CHOICE HOTELS
www.choicehotels.com

COURTYARD BY MARRIOTT
www.courtyard.marriott.com

CROWNE PLAZA HOTELS
www.ihg.com/crowneplaza

DOUBLETREE BY HILTON
www.doubletree.com

EMBASSY SUITES BY HILTON
www.embassysuites.com

FAIRMONT
www.fairmont.com

FOUR SEASONS
www.fourseasons.com

HAMPTON BY HILTON
www.hampton.com

HILTON HOTELS & RESORTS
www.hilton.com

HOLIDAY INN
www.holidayinn.com

HYATT
www.hyatt.com

INTERCONTINENTAL HOTELS & RESORTS
www.intercontinental.com

KIMPTON HOTELS & RESTAURANTS
www.kimptonhotels.com

LE MERIDIEN
www.lemeridien.com

LOEWS HOTELS
www.loewshotels.com

MARRIOTT
www.marriott.com

OMNI HOTELS
www.omnihotels.com

RAMADA WORLDWIDE
www.ramada.com

RENAISSANCE
http://renaissance-hotels.marriott.com

RESIDENCE INN BY MARRIOTT
www.residenceinn.com

RITZ CARLTON
www.ritzcarlton.com

SHERATON
www.sheraton.com

TAJ
www.tajhotels.com

WESTIN HOTELS & RESORTS
www.westin.com

WYNDHAM
www.wyndham.com

Index

See also Accommodations and Restaurant indexes, below.

Photo Credits

Notes

Notes